My Jewish Year

Celebrating Our Holidays

Dedicated with love to Rosalie Shaffer, Eileen Fisher,
and Rachel Fisher (my mother-in-law, wife, and daughter),
three generations of extraordinary teachers, with whom
I have shared the joy of these festivals.

And, to Harvey Witman, the superlative Educational Director of
Temple Isaiah Religious School, its fine staff, and the wonderful
children with whom I have been privileged to work.

To Adam Siegel, the editor of this book, my deep thanks and
appreciation for his graciousness, skill, and support.

PROJECT EDITOR: ADAM SIEGEL

BOOK DESIGN: ROBERT J. O'DELL

ARTISTS: CARYN KING, LARRY NOLTE, CLARE SIEFFERT

The editor and publisher thank Rabbi Jeffrey Sirkman for
his insightful editorial assistance.

The editor and publisher gratefully acknowledge the cooperation of the following source of photographs for this book:

Bill Aron Photography, **18, 40, 52, 63, 72, 111;** Michah Bar-Am/Magnum, **50;** Paul Barton/The Stock Market, **47, 153;** John Carter/Photo Researchers Inc., **25;** Sandy Clark/The Stock Market, **7;** Jim Cron/Monkmeyer, **21;** P. Dawalt/Explorer/Photo Researchers Inc., **90;** Jose Fernandez/Woodfin Camp and Assoc. **22;** J.I. Greenberg/Photo Researchers Inc., **155;** Geoffrey Hiller, **101;** Tana Hobin, **151;** The Jerusalem Publishing House, **152;** Jewish National Fund, **89, 93;** Kagan/Monkmeyer, **27;** Richard Lobell/Travel Source, **138, 141, 143;** Tom McCarthy/The Stock Market, **34;** Roy Morsch/The Stock Market, **56;** Garo Nalbandian/Biblical Archaeology Society, **38;** Robert J. O'Dell, **134;** Gabe Palmer/The Stock Market, **11;** April Saul, **67, 118, 124;** Chuck Savage/The Stock Market, **96;** Blair Seitz/Photo Researchers Inc. **31;** Frank Siteman/Monkmeyer Press, **131;** J. Gerald Smith/Photo Researchers Inc. **32;** Jeffrey D. Smith/Woodfin Camp and Assoc. **148;** Illana Weber, **137;** Vicki L. Weber, **95;** Michael Weisbrot and Family, **60;** David Wells, **69.**

ADAM FISHER

My Jewish Year

Celebrating Our Holidays

BEHRMAN HOUSE, INC.

CONTENTS

Tishre 1 תִּשְׁרֵי

Ḥeshvan חֶשְׁוָן

Kislev כִּסְלֵו

Tevet טֵבֵת

Shevat שְׁבָט

Adar אֲדָר

Nisan נִיסָן

Iyar אִיָּר

Sivan סִיוָן

Tammuz תַּמּוּז

Av אָב

Elul אֱלוּל

ROSH

Everyone has a birthday. Your parents, your teacher, your best friend, even your dog has a birthday. But did you know that the world has a birthday too?

Renew us for a year that is good and sweet.

MAḤZOR: ROSH HASHANAH LITURGY

HASHANAH

ראֹשׁ הַשָּׁנָה

Long, long ago,
before there were people,
before there were animals,
before there were seas and stars
and sky, God created the world.

God made tall green trees to
give us shade.
God made soft grass to tickle our toes
when we walk barefoot.
God made red and purple and yellow
flowers with sweet smells.
And God lifted up the mountains so
tall that they touch the clouds.

Jewish people remember the birthday of the world. We thank God for creating the world by celebrating a holy day called Rosh Hashanah.

A DAY OF REMEMBERING

Rosh Hashanah marks the beginning of a new year. Just as you are one year older on your birthday, the world is one year older on this holy day.

The Hebrew words "Rosh Hashanah" mean "Head of the Year." Our Jewish year begins on the first day of the Hebrew month called **Tishre**.

WHAT ARE YOU THANKFUL FOR?

On Rosh Hashanah we thank God for the people who love us when we are sad, who take care of us when we are sick, who forgive us when we make a mistake, and who teach us new things when we need help.

Can you draw a picture or write about someone you are thankful for?

A YEAR
TO REMEMBER

On Rosh Hashanah we look at the things we have done during the past year. This chart will help you to remember.

My name is

_____

I am _____ years old.

Our Jewish year is 57_____

I am proud that I _____

_____

_____

I am sorry that I _____

_____

_____

I will try to do better next year by

_____

_____

Summer has ended.
The leaves on the trees are changing.
They turn from green to red
and orange.
A new Jewish year is about to begin.

Rosh Hashanah is a time to remember. This holiday is called a "Day of Remembering," in Hebrew, **Yom Hazikaron**. On this special day we remember the year that has passed. Have we done good deeds? Are there some things we wish we had done better?

Another name for Rosh Hashanah is "Day of Judgment," or in Hebrew, **Yom Hadin**. It is said that God keeps a book with every person's name in it. In this way, we are held responsible for all the things we do.

Rosh Hashanah is a day of hope. We hope for good things in the year to come.

A child whose grandmother is sick hopes that she will be well. A child whose parents are looking for a job hopes they will soon find work. Some children might hope that their friend won't move away. Whatever people hope for, they can tell their hopes to God.

It's fun to see how many inches we've grown. But on Rosh Hashanah we measure something else. We measure ourselves on the inside. We think about how we acted during the year that is ending so we can behave better in the next.

AT HOME

Rosh Hashanah begins in the evening. We put on our best clothes and enjoy a holiday meal with family and friends.

WHAT IS IT?

Connect the dots to see something we eat each year at Rosh Hashanah.

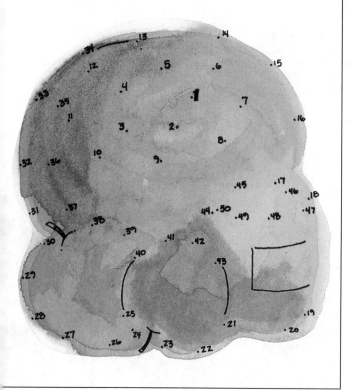

We light the candles and say a blessing to welcome the New Year:

בָּרוּךְ אַתָּה יְיָ אֱלֹהֵינוּ מֶלֶךְ הָעוֹלָם אֲשֶׁר קִדְּשָׁנוּ בְּמִצְוֹתָיו וְצִוָּנוּ לְהַדְלִיק נֵר שֶׁל יוֹם טוֹב.

Blessed are You, Adonai our God, Ruler of the world, who makes us holy with mitzvot, and commands us to kindle the festival lights.

We also recite the **Sheheḥeyanu.** This blessing thanks God for life and for allowing us to reach the New Year:

בָּרוּךְ אַתָּה יְיָ אֱלֹהֵינוּ מֶלֶךְ הָעוֹלָם שֶׁהֶחֱיָנוּ וְקִיְּמָנוּ וְהִגִּיעָנוּ לַזְּמַן הַזֶּה.

Blessed are You, Adonai our God, Ruler of the world, who has given us life, sustained us, and brought us to this season of joy.

On the table is a loaf of ḥallah bread. The ḥallah we usually eat is baked in a long braid. But on Rosh Hashanah the bread is round. It looks like the crown kings and queens wear. On Rosh Hashanah we remember that God rules the world.

A SWEET YEAR

We tear off a piece of the golden ḥallah and dip it in honey to make it sweet.

Sometimes the ḥallah has raisins, which make it even sweeter.

We also eat apples dipped in honey, because we hope we will have a sweet year. We hope that people will be kind to one another, and we hope that we will all be healthy and happy. We say, "May the New Year be a sweet one."

NEW YEAR CARDS

On Rosh Hashanah we wish everyone a happy new year. We say the Hebrew words, "Shanah Tovah"(שָׁנָה טוֹבָה), a good year. We send Rosh Hashanah cards to those who live far away.

Some people buy cards in a store, but some of the best cards are the ones we make ourselves.

SHANAH TOVAH

Decorate this Rosh Hashanah card to show how good we hope the coming year will be.

IN THE SYNAGOGUE

We welcome the New Year in the synagogue. When we walk into the synagogue it will be filled with people.

You will see the Torah. It will have a white cover, and a silver crown called a *keter*. Some Torah scrolls have two smaller silver crowns called *rimonim*.

People will carry the Torah around the synagogue. Then someone will read from it in Hebrew. You may not understand the words yet, but they sound beautiful.

WHAT'S IN A NAME?

The Jewish New Year has many names.

On the line after each name fill in the number of the meaning below.

NAME

Yom Hazikaron_____

Yom Hadin_____

Rosh Hashanah_____

Yom Teruah_____

MEANING

1 Head of the year

2 Day of sounding the shofar

3 A day to think about the year that is ending

4 A day when God judges us

THE SHOFAR

During morning prayers we hear the sound of the **shofar** (שׁוֹפָר). The shofar is made from the horn of a male sheep, a ram. The shofar is hollow, and when it is blown the sound is sharp and loud. Rosh Hashanah is also called **Yom Teruah,** "The Day of Sounding the Shofar."

The shofar reminds us of events that happened long ago. The shofar was sounded at Mount Sinai when the Jewish people promised to obey God's commandments. The sound of the ram's horn reminds us to keep that promise.

The shofar makes four special sounds:

    tekiah, the sound of telling people to pay attention;

    teruah, the sound of calling people together;

    shevarim, the sounds of different hopes people have for a good year;

    tekiah gedolah, the sound of people welcoming the New Year.

TRUE OR FALSE

Fill in the **T** if the sentence is true.
Fill in the **F** if the sentence is false.

1. On Rosh Hashanah we dip cookies in milk. T F

2. The shofar reminds us to obey God's commandments. T F

3. On Rosh Hashanah the ḥallah is round. T F

4. The shofar is made from a car's horn. T F

5. The Hebrew words Shanah Tovah mean "Happy Birthday." T F

6. Rosh Hashanah is the Jewish New Year. T F

TASHLICH

After Rosh Hashanah services in the synagogue, many people go to a nearby stream or river. We turn our pockets inside out to empty them of crumbs. We drop the crumbs into the water and watch them float away. It is like throwing away the bad things we may have done. We make ourselves clean for the start of a fresh year.

MY HOLIDAY DICTIONARY

ROSH HASHANAH means "Head of the Year"—on this day we celebrate the beginning of the new Jewish year

SHANAH TOVAH we wish everyone a good year with these Hebrew words

SHEHEḤEYANU the blessing which thanks God for life, and for allowing us to reach the present moment

SHOFAR the horn of a ram that is blown on Rosh Hashanah

TASHLICH after Rosh Hashanah services we go to a nearby stream or river to empty our pockets of crumbs; we are throwing away the bad things we have done and making ourselves clean for the start of a fresh year

TISHRE we celebrate Rosh Hashanah on the first day of the Hebrew month Tishre

YOM HADIN means "Day of Judgment"— on Rosh Hashanah God judges our actions of the past year

YOM HAZIKARON another name for Rosh Hashanah, means "Day of Remembering"—on Rosh Hashanah we remember the year that has passed

YOM TERUAH means the "Day of Sounding the Shofar"— on Rosh Hashanah we blow the shofar to welcome the New Year

Tishre 10 תִּשְׁרֵי

Ḥeshvan חֶשְׁוָן

Kislev כִּסְלֵו

Tevet טֵבֵת

Shevat שְׁבָט

Adar אֲדָר

Nisan נִיסָן

Iyar אִיָּר

Sivan סִיוָן

Tammuz תַּמּוּז

Av אָב

Elul אֱלוּל

YOM

We try to be kind. We try to help our friends. We try to listen to our parents. And most of the time we do.

But sometimes we do things that hurt other people. We may not be able to see the hurt on the outside, but it is on the inside, where only they can feel it.

Forgive and pardon our sins on this Day of Atonement.

MAḤZOR: YOM KIPPUR CONFESSIONAL

KIPPUR

יוֹם כִּפּוּר

We always try to do the right thing, just as a person shooting an arrow aims to hit the target. But sometimes we "miss the mark." We don't hit the bull's eye every time. The word for "sin" in Hebrew is **ḥet**, which means to miss the mark.

We may not tell the truth—and that can hurt. And we may make fun of someone— that always hurts.

After we hurt someone it can be hard to say "I'm sorry." And even though saying it can't erase what we did, it can make us and the person we hurt feel a whole lot better.

_____

_____

_____

_____

_____

THE TEN DAYS OF REPENTANCE

On Rosh Hashanah we begin to think about how we acted during the past year. Even though we did many good things, we are sorry we did not do more. We want to ask forgiveness from God for the wrong things we have done.

MISSING THE MARK

When were some of the times this past year that you "missed the mark"? Write on each line the things you did that hurt others.

23

But before we can ask God to forgive us, we must try to make up for what we did wrong and apologize to those we have hurt. This is called **teshuvah**, or repentance.

For ten days, we say we are sorry to all the people we have treated unfairly or unkindly. We ask for forgiveness.

COUNT THE DAYS

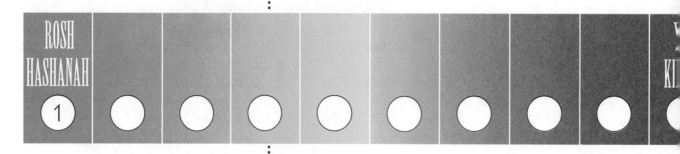

In each box number the days from Rosh Hashanah to Yom Kippur.

These ten days are called **Aseret Y'mei Teshuvah**, the Ten Days of Repentance.

THE DAY OF ATONEMENT

On the tenth day after Rosh Hashanah, we ask for forgiveness from God. We call this day Yom Kippur. The words Yom Kippur mean "Day of Atonement."

Atonement happens when we try to become "at one" with God. We tell God that we are sorry. We ask God to forgive us. We promise to try to do better in the coming new year. And so we move closer to God and to the people we love.

Did you notice the two words in atonement which tell us what the word means?

Write them here

_____

TESHUVAH

Repentance, or teshuvah, happens not only because we say we are sorry, but because we try to make up for what we did wrong.

Something that was taken can be returned. Something that was broken can be fixed.

Think of something you can fix or repair that begins with each letter in the word teshuvah.

T _____

E _____

S _____

H _____

U _____

V _____

A _____

H _____

God wants us to be good to one another. God wants us to take care of each other. So when we hurt someone it is important to tell God and that person that we are sorry.

It is not always easy to forgive someone who hurts us. But Jewish tradition teaches that when we do, our own sins are forgiven as well.

AT HOME

Yom Kippur begins at home. After eating a good meal, we light the holiday candles. We also light another candle called a memorial or **yahrzeit candle.** The yahrzeit candle helps us to remember people we love who are no longer alive.

The yahrzeit candle is not placed in a candlestick. It comes in a glass. It will burn for the entire holiday, for at least twenty-four hours.

On Yom Kippur afternoon there is a special service in the synagogue called **Yizkor** to remember people who have died.

FASTING

Adults do not eat anything, or even drink anything, on Yom Kippur. They feel so sorry for the things they have done wrong that they **fast** for the whole day. Fasting helps them to think

The yahrzeit candle burns for twenty-four hours. We light the candle on Yom Kippur and on the anniversary of someone's death. It helps us to remember someone we love.

about how they can become better people in the year to come. Anyone who is sick, or very young or very old, does not have to fast on Yom Kippur.

KOL NIDRE

On Yom Kippur we spend most of the day in the synagogue. The rabbi and the cantor wear white robes. And the Torah scrolls have white covers to show that we want a fresh, clean start in the new year.

Each of us depends on other people—for food, clothing, friendship, and love. On Yom Kippur we remind ourselves to answer when someone asks for our help.

On Yom Kippur we read the Book of Jonah. This story teaches that God is always ready to forgive.

The Yom Kippur service begins in the evening with a famous prayer called **Kol Nidre**. Sometimes we make promises without first thinking if we can really keep them. During the year we may make promises to God that we cannot keep. The Kol Nidre prayer frees us from those promises to God.

As the cantor chants the sad and beautiful melody of Kol Nidre, we listen with our ears and with our hearts.

AL ḤET

During the service we read an important prayer called **Al Ḥet**. Do you remember what the word "ḥet" means?

In the Al Ḥet prayer we confess our sins as a group. As Jews, we must accept responsibility not only for ourselves, but for the entire community.

We have all done things we are sorry about. So we say the prayer together—men and women, girls and boys. We tell God we are sorry not only for what we have done wrong, but for the things our family, friends, and neighbors have done wrong too.

MISSING WORDS

One word is missing in each sentence. Write the correct word to complete the sentence. (Choose from the words in the circles below.)

1. _____ means that we try to feel "at one" with God by saying we are sorry for the bad things we have done.

2. At home we light _____ candles in memory of those who have died.

3. During the Yom Kippur service we listen to a beautiful prayer that is sung called

_____.

4. There are _____ days between Rosh Hashanah and Yom Kippur.

5. _____ is a prayer that tells the bad things we have done.

6. Grownups do not eat or drink on Yom Kippur. They _____.

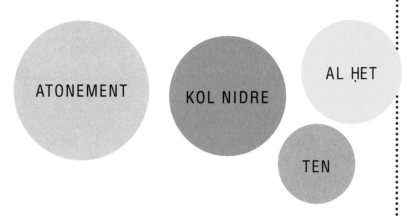

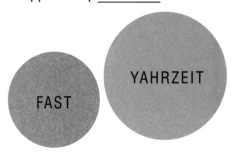

WHAT CAN YOU DO?

What could you do to make the world better? Draw a picture or write about something that would help make someone happier.

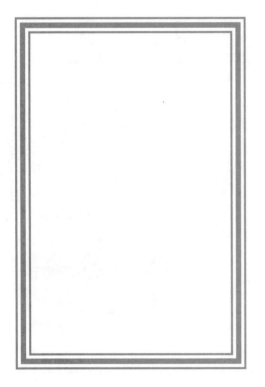

We say the Al Ḥet out loud so that everyone can hear. Some people tap their chests with their fists as they mention each sin. It is a way of showing how sorry they are.

Many times during the Yom Kippur service we sing a special prayer called *Avinu Malkenu*. The prayer asks God to forgive us and to treat us kindly, even though we don't always act the way we should.

BREAKING THE FAST

On Yom Kippur day, people pray and study from early morning until dark. In some synagogues, the service lasts until we can see three stars in the night sky.

We blow the shofar only once on Yom Kippur. The **tekiah gedolah**, the one long blast of the ram's horn, tells us that this holy day has come to an end. The last sound of the shofar wishes everyone a good new year.

After the blowing of the shofar, family and friends share a "break the fast" meal. It is nice to invite people who might be alone to come to your home to break the fast with your family. Often people eat bagels, lox, cheese, and other tasty foods.

This is a happy time when everyone enjoys eating together. We feel there is a new beginning for us. And we feel cleansed of all the things we have done wrong.

A very long and loud blast of the shofar signals the end of Yom Kippur.

MAKING THE WORLD A BETTER PLACE

On Yom Kippur we look back at the year that has passed, and we look ahead to the new year that has just begun. We feel clean and good and full of hope. We have made a new start. We know that we can be better people in the new year. And we hope the new year will be good for all people everywhere.

On Yom Kippur, we think of the many things in our world we would like to make better. People are hungry, people don't have jobs, people are treated unfairly. And we want to heal those hurts.

A cup of tea tastes sweeter when it is shared with someone who cares.

We think of the things we can do to help other people. We can feed the hungry, visit people who are sick, and help our friends at school. We can give money to the poor, money to help Israel, and money to people who try to make the world better.

All of these are acts of **tzedakah** (צְדָקָה). Tzedakah is our Jewish way of helping others.

MY HOLIDAY DICTIONARY

AL ḤET a prayer which Jews recite together to confess our sins

ASERET Y'MEI TESHUVAH the ten days between Rosh Hashanah and Yom Kippur when we apologize to the people we have hurt (The Ten Days of Repentance)

DAY OF ATONEMENT Yom Kippur is called the Day of Atonement, a time when we try to become "at one" with God

FASTING not eating or drinking on Yom Kippur to show how sorry we are

ḤET Hebrew for the word sin, which means to miss the mark

KOL NIDRE the ancient prayer that is chanted on the evening of Yom Kippur—the prayer frees us from promises made to God that we could not keep during the year

TEKIAH GEDOLAH the last blast of the shofar, which marks the end of Yom Kippur

TESHUVAH repentance, which happens not only when we say we are sorry to someone we have hurt, but when we try to make up for what we did wrong

TZEDAKAH things we do to help others—feed the hungry, give money to the poor, visit people who are sick

YAHRZEIT CANDLE we light this candle to remember someone who is no longer alive

YIZKOR a service on Yom Kippur to help us remember people who have died

Tishre 15 תִּשְׁרֵי

Ḥeshvan חֶשְׁוָן

Kislev כִּסְלֵו

Tevet טֵבֵת

Shevat שְׁבָט

Adar אֲדָר

Nisan נִיסָן

Iyar אִיָּר

Sivan סִיוָן

Tammuz תַּמּוּז

Av אָב

Elul אֱלוּל

You shall live in huts seven days...
in order that future generations
may know that I made the
Israelites live in huts when
I brought them out of Egypt.

LEVITICUS 23: 42,43

SUKKOT

סֻכּוֹת

When you eat a peanut butter and jelly sandwich, you know that a farmer grew the wheat for the bread, the peanuts for the peanut butter, and the grapes for the jelly.

But farmers don't make the soil and the sun and the rain that makes all things grow. For those things we must thank God.

So at the end of the summer, when juicy apples, crunchy carrots, ears of corn, and all the other fruits and vegetables have been gathered from the fields, we thank God with a joyous celebration—the holiday of Sukkot.

SUKKOT IN THE FIELDS

Help each farmer build a sukkah by drawing small huts in the field.

HOW SUKKOT GOT ITS NAME

Thousands of years ago, most Jewish people were farmers. In the fall, the grapes on the vine were bursting with juice. The grain stood tall in the field and the olives hung ripe on the trees. It was time to harvest the crops.

The food had to be gathered quickly. So the farmers built little booths or huts in the fields where they worked. They slept in these huts so that they could begin the harvest early in the morning. They could pick the crops until the stars appeared in the dark night sky.

The holiday of Sukkot is named after these little booths. Sukkot is the Hebrew word for "booths."

When the food was finally gathered and safely stored, it was time to thank God. This was one of the three festivals when the farmers and their families climbed the hills to Jerusalem. That is why Sukkot is one of the three pilgrimage festivals, called *shalosh regalim*. A pilgrimage is a journey to a holy place.

The farmers brought sheep and goats to give to God. They brought gifts of flour and wine to the Temple.

PILGRIMAGE MAZE

Help the farmers bring their gifts to Jerusalem.

There was a wonderful festival in Jerusalem. Musicians played joyful music on harps, drums, and flutes. The people danced and sang and thanked God for the harvest.

WANDERING IN THE DESERT

The Torah tells us there was another time when our ancestors lived in huts. After the People of Israel were freed from slavery in Egypt, they wandered in the desert for forty years. During their long wandering they built little huts to protect them from the cold desert nights.

HOW WE BUILD A SUKKAH

Today, most of us do not grow and pick our own food. And we do not sleep in the fields during the harvest time. But we are thankful for all that God gives us.

Some Bedouin Arabs in Israel still live in tents in the desert, just as our ancestors did thousands of years ago.

So every fall we build a **sukkah**, just like the farmers built in ancient Israel.

A sukkah has four walls and a roof made of corn stalks. Some people use green pine branches. They smell good. When you go into the sukkah and look up, you'll see the sky peeking through the branches.

Some families build a sukkah in the back yard. Those who live in the city build it on the terrace or roof of their apartment houses.

You can decorate the walls of the sukkah with photographs from Israel or pictures that you draw yourself.

You can hang many different things from the ceiling of the sukkah—sweet smelling flowers, dark purple eggplants, yellow squash, red apples, and funny-shaped gourds.

Some people save their New Year's cards from Rosh Hashanah and use them to decorate the sukkah. Mothers, fathers, sisters, brothers, and friends can all help.

WHAT WE DO IN THE SUKKAH

At the beginning of Sukkot we have a special holiday meal in the sukkah.

When we enter the sukkah we say a blessing:

בָּרוּךְ אַתָּה יְיָ אֱלֹהֵינוּ מֶלֶךְ הָעוֹלָם
אֲשֶׁר קִדְּשָׁנוּ בְּמִצְוֹתָיו וְצִוָּנוּ
לֵישֵׁב בַּסֻּכָּה.

Blessed are You, Adonai our God, Ruler of the world, who makes us holy with mitzvot, and commands us to dwell in the sukkah.

Tie a string tightly around an apple's stem and it's ready to hang from the roof of the sukkah.

We light the candles and recite the holiday Kiddush, the blessing over wine.

Even if you don't have a sukkah, you can still say the blessings when you eat the holiday meal inside your home.

The Sukkot holiday lasts for a whole week. During this time try to eat as many meals in the sukkah as you can. Some people even sleep in the sukkah. If you do, make sure you have plenty of blankets in case it gets cold at night.

WELCOMING GUESTS

It's important to share Sukkot with other people. Cousins, friends, and neighbors can visit, eat, and even sleep in your sukkah. This is called welcoming guests, **hachnasat orḥim**.

DECORATE THE SUKKAH

Here is a sukkah for you to decorate. Hang fruits and vegetables in it to make it as beautiful as you can.

41

THE LULAV AND THE ETROG

Sukkot services are held in the synagogue. We wave the **lulav** and **etrog** there, as well as in the sukkah.

The lulav has three parts: The long, thin part is a palm branch. The shorter branches are from a myrtle bush and a willow tree.

The etrog looks like a big lemon, but it smells sweet and delicious.

We take the lulav in our right hand and the etrog in our left hand and bring them together. We shake the lulav. And we point the lulav and etrog in every direction. This shows that God is everywhere.

Some say the palm leaf, which is long and thin, stands for our spines; the myrtle leaf, which is round, stands for our eyes; and the willow leaf, which is oval, stands for our mouths. The etrog, they say, stands for our hearts.

So when you wave the lulav and etrog you are thanking God with your whole body.

As we wave the lulav and etrog we say a blessing of thanks to God:

בָּרוּךְ אַתָּה יְיָ
אֱלֹהֵינוּ מֶלֶךְ הָעוֹלָם
אֲשֶׁר קִדְּשָׁנוּ בְּמִצְוֹתָיו
וְצִוָּנוּ עַל נְטִילַת לוּלָב.

Blessed are You, Adonai our God, Ruler of the world, who makes us holy with mitzvot, and commands us to wave the lulav.

In the synagogue the Torah is read. It tells how our ancestors celebrated Sukkot long ago, and how we can celebrate it today. We say special prayers of thanks called **Hallel**.

GIVING TO OTHERS

God gave the earth to all people, and God wants everyone to have enough food. So another way we thank God

When you go to the synagogue on Sukkot, you will be able to hold the lulav and the etrog.

MISSING LETTERS

Two letters are missing in each word. Write the letters to complete the name of each object.

L◯L A◯

◯T◯O G

◯A◯M

WI◯L◯W

◯UKK◯H

M◯RT◯E

for all that we have is to give food to those who do not have enough to eat. You can bring cans and boxes of food to a special food bank. Your synagogue may collect food for the poor. Or, you can give money to groups that help feed the hungry.

At the end of Sukkot we celebrate **Shemini Atzeret.** On this day we pray for winter rain to prepare the ground for spring planting. Some Jews set aside a special day for Shemini Atzeret, while others combine it with Simḥat Torah.

Sukkot is a time to be happy. We are grateful for all the good things God gives to us. And we share our food and friendship with others. Sukkot is such a happy time that this festival is even called the "Time of Our Happiness," **Z'man Simḥataynu.**

So we wish one another **"Ḥag Samayaḥ,"** Happy Holiday!

44

MY HOLIDAY DICTIONARY

ETROG a yellow, lemon-like fruit that smells sweet

HACHNASAT ORḤIM Hebrew for "welcoming guests"—on Sukkot we invite friends, relatives, and neighbors to our sukkah

ḤAG SAMAYAḤ Hebrew for "happy holiday"

HALLEL prayers of thanks that we recite on Sukkot and other holidays

LULAV the combination of palm, willow, and myrtle branches

SHEMINI ATZERET the day at the end of Sukkot when we pray for winter rains

SUKKAH a hut we build on Sukkot to remind us of the time when our ancestors lived in them

Z'MAN SIMḤATAYNU another name for Sukkot which means "Time of Our Happiness"

Tishre תִּשְׁרֵי

Heshvan חֶשְׁוָן

Kislev כִּסְלֵו

Tevet טֵבֵת

Shevat שְׁבָט

Adar אֲדָר

Nisan נִיסָן

Iyar אִיָּר

Sivan סִיוָן

Tammuz תַּמּוּז

Av אָב

Elul אֱלוּל

Turn it (the Torah) again and again, for everything is in it.

AVOT 2:8

When you finish reading a favorite book, do you wish there was more to read? Or maybe you enjoyed it so much that you start to read it all over again.

Some people feel that way about family albums, with pictures of parents and grandparents, and maybe even great grandparents. They love to look at the pictures and hear the stories.

And that is how we feel about our Torah, the family album for the whole Jewish people.

SIMHAT TORAH

שִׂמְחַת תּוֹרָה

WHY WE LOVE THE TORAH

The Torah (תּוֹרָה) is God's most precious gift to us. It has stories we all love to read. The Torah tells us how God created the world. It tells us about Adam and Eve in the Garden of Eden. And it tells us about Noah and his huge ark.

The Torah also tells us the history of our people. We relive the adventures of Abraham and Sarah. We read about Joseph and his colorful coat. And we learn how Moses brought our people out of Egypt to the Land of Israel. Torah is the story of the love between God and our people.

But there is even more. The Torah teaches us how to be Jewish. God's commandments, the **mitzvot** (מִצְוֹת), show us how to lead good and honest lives.

There is so much to learn that some

people spend their whole lives studying the Torah.

BEGINNING AGAIN

The Torah is so important to us that as soon as we finish reading it, we go right back to the beginning. We start reading the Torah all over again. We even have a special holiday to show our love for the Torah. It is called Simḥat Torah, which means "Joy in the Torah." We celebrate Simḥat Torah at the end of the Sukkot festival.

TRUE OR FALSE

Fill in the **T** if the sentence is true.
Fill in the **F** if the sentence is false.

1. The Torah contains the history of the Jewish People.   T   F

2. Adam and Eve led the People of Israel out of Egypt.   T   F

3. The Torah teaches us how to lead good lives.   T   F

4. Abraham and Sarah had a huge ark.   T   F

5. We celebrate our love for the Torah on Simḥat Torah.   T   F

THE TORAH SCROLL

Most books are printed on paper that is made from trees. The ink is pressed onto the paper by printing machines. But the Torah is different. It is not printed like a regular book.

The Torah is written by hand, using the point of a feather dipped in black ink. The feather usually comes from a turkey. The person who writes the Torah is called a **sofer**, or scribe.

The sofer writes the Torah on pieces of parchment. Parchment is made from the skin of an animal—usually a sheep. Many pieces of

parchment are sewn together and rolled up to make a scroll.

If you unrolled a Torah scroll, you would see just how long it really is. Some are so long they stretch 150 feet. That's equal to 12 cars lined up end to end.

The letters of the Torah look very beautiful because they are written with love.

BE A SCRIBE

Fill in the Hebrew letters to see the first word in the Torah

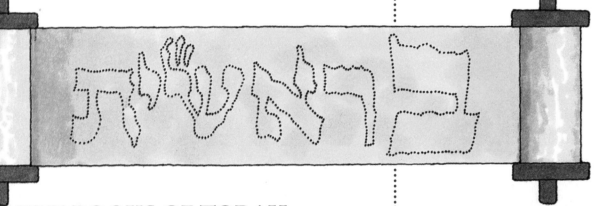

FIVE BOOKS OF TORAH

Sometimes we open up a gift box and we find two or three presents inside. The Torah is like that. The long scroll

There are many books in the Bible. The first five books are called the Torah. You can see them on the left. What are their names? How many books are there in the whole Bible?

has not one but five books written on it. The five books in the Torah are: Genesis (בְּרֵאשִׁית), Exodus (שְׁמוֹת), Leviticus (וַיִּקְרָא), Numbers (בַּמִּדְבָּר), and Deuteronomy (דְּבָרִים).

The Torah is kept in the Holy Ark, or **Aron Hakodesh**. Every week a different portion of the Torah is read aloud. Each time we begin a new part of the Torah it is like opening another wonderful present. It takes one year to read the whole Torah.

On the holiday of Simḥat Torah we come to the end of the Torah scroll.

We read the very last words of the Torah and then we turn all the way back to the beginning to read the very first words, "In the beginning...."

IN THE SYNAGOGUE

Everyone loves a parade. And on Simḥat Torah you can march in a special parade in the synagogue. During the service the Torah scrolls are taken from the Holy Ark. They are carried around the synagogue in parades called **hakkafot**. People who carry the scrolls hold them very carefully, as if they were holding a baby.

JOIN THE PARADE

Decorate this flag for Simhat Torah by drawing a picture from the Bible on it.

You can join the parade too. You can wave a Simhat Torah flag. You can even make your own. As the Torah passes we touch and kiss it to show how much we love God's words.

JOY IN THE TORAH

Sometimes we are so happy that we want to dance. That's the way we feel on Simhat Torah. You can join the circle, hold hands, and dance around and around.

Afterwards we eat cookies and sticky jelly apples. Everyone is happy. We wish each other a happy holiday – "Hag Samayah."

We see smiles on every face and hear happiness in every voice. That is what Simhat Torah means – Joy in the Torah.

MY HOLIDAY DICTIONARY

ARON HAKODESH the "Holy Ark," the place where the Torah is kept in the synagogue

HAKKAFOT the parades on Simḥat Torah when the Torah scrolls are carried around the synagogue

MITZVOT God's laws, which show us how to lead good and honest lives

SOFER the person who writes a Torah using a feather dipped in ink

Sunday   יוֹם רִאשׁוֹן

Monday   יוֹם שֵׁנִי

Tuesday   יוֹם שְׁלִישִׁי

Wednesday   יוֹם רְבִיעִי

Thursday   יוֹם חֲמִישִׁי

Friday   יוֹם שִׁשִׁי

Shabbat   שַׁבָּת

And God blessed the seventh day...

GENESIS 2:3

שַׁבָּת

SHABBAT

When you finish a beautiful painting, you like to sit back and look at what you have done. You are proud of it, you enjoy it, and you want others to enjoy it too. When God finished creating the world, God was very pleased. So God set aside a day to enjoy the world—the holy day Shabbat.

Every seven days we celebrate this special day. To find out why, let's begin by reading a story from the Torah. It tells us how the world was created.

CREATION

In the beginning there was only darkness and emptiness.

Then God created light.

On the second day God created the sky.

On the third day God made the land and the sea.

On the fourth day God created the sun, the moon, and the stars.

On the fifth day God made the fish that swim and the birds that fly.

And on the sixth day God created all the animals and man and woman.

For six days God worked. And on the seventh day God rested. God blessed the seventh day and made it holy. So every seventh day–every Saturday–is a holy day.

That seventh day is called Shabbat, the day of rest for God, for people, and even for animals.

LOOKING BACK

Shabbat is one of our oldest holidays. It is the only holiday mentioned in the Ten Commandments: "Observe the Sabbath day and keep it holy."

Long ago, the shofar was blown to announce the end of the week. People were happy to hear the sound of the shofar. They had worked hard for six days.

Today in Israel there are still places where the shofar is blown to announce the beginning of Shabbat.

When the Jews heard the shofar, they knew that Shabbat would soon begin. They hurried home from the fields, dusty and tired. They washed and put on fresh, clean clothes. Then they ate a special dinner.

On Shabbat, no one worked. People  did not farm or cook or build. Shabbat was a day to study and to pray and to rest.

SHABBAT EVENING AT HOME

When you finish your homework and chores, what do you like to do?

We begin preparing for Shabbat on Friday. We polish the silver wine cup and candlesticks until they shine. We cover the table with a white cloth and place a bowl of fresh flowers in the center. Soup simmers on the stove and potatoes brown in the oven. We are ready to welcome Shabbat.

SABBATH SPICE

Many years ago there was a Roman emperor who loved to eat. The emperor was friendly with a rabbi who loved to cook.

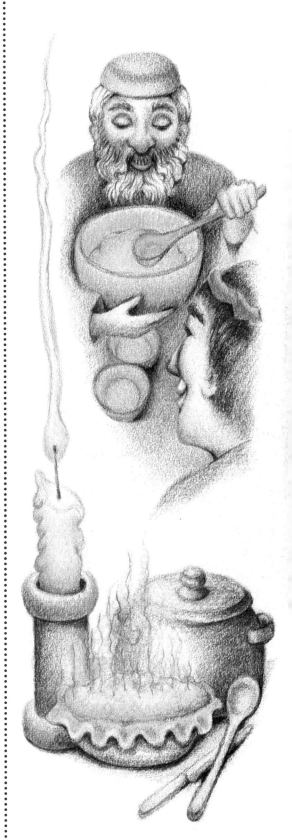

The rabbi invited the emperor to dinner on Shabbat. They ate a splendid meal of soup and vegetables and fish. For dessert the rabbi served the most delicious pie the emperor had ever tasted. When the emperor was finished, he thanked the rabbi and asked for the recipes. The rabbi was happy to give them to him.

During the week the emperor's cook prepared all the recipes, but the emperor was disappointed. He complained to the rabbi, "The food does not taste as good as it did in your house on Shabbat."

"Of course not," replied the rabbi. "The food did not have the Sabbath spice."

"But what is this Sabbath spice?" asked the emperor. "Where can I buy it?"

The rabbi replied, "My friend, you cannot buy it. The Sabbath spice comes from the special feeling of peace and rest on Shabbat which makes all food taste so much better!"

CANDLES

Shabbat begins with the lighting of candles. On Friday, before the sun sets, we light at least two candles. Some people light one for each person in the family.

After we light the candles we recite a blessing:

בָּרוּךְ אַתָּה יְיָ אֱלֹהֵינוּ מֶלֶךְ הָעוֹלָם אֲשֶׁר קִדְּשָׁנוּ בְּמִצְוֹתָיו וְצִוָּנוּ לְהַדְלִיק נֵר שֶׁל שַׁבָּת.

Blessed are You, Adonai our God, Ruler of the world, who makes us holy with mitzvot, and commands us to kindle the Sabbath lights.

Many people add an extra prayer asking God to watch over their family and friends.

Parents bless their children:

May God bless and keep you.
May God's light shine on you and be good to you.
May God's light shine on you and give you peace.

If you light a Shabbat candle for everyone in your house, how many candles would you light? Draw them below. Then write an extra personal prayer to say after lighting the Shabbat candles.

MY PRAYER

_____
_____
_____
_____
_____
_____
_____

KIDDUSH

On Friday evening we recite the **Kiddush** (קִדּוּשׁ), a prayer which tells everyone that the Sabbath is a holy day. The word "Kiddush" means "holiness."

The Kiddush has three parts:

The first part tells us that after God finished creating the world, God blessed the world and rested.

The second part of the Kiddush is the blessing for the sweet red wine we will sip:

בָּרוּךְ אַתָּה יְיָ אֱלֹהֵינוּ מֶלֶךְ הָעוֹלָם
בּוֹרֵא פְּרִי הַגָּפֶן.

Blessed are You, Adonai our God, Ruler of the world, Creator of the fruit of the vine.

The third part of the Kiddush reminds us of our Exodus from Egypt, when God freed us from slavery and led us to the Land of Israel.

On Shabbat we are free to enjoy the world God has created.

המוציא לחם מן הארץ

ḤALLAH

Long ago, people ate dark bread with their meals during the week. But on Shabbat they ate ḥallah (חַלָּה), a tasty bread made with eggs and white flour. Today we still enjoy this braided soft bread.

Before eating the ḥallah, some families have a special ceremony of washing hands just as the priests did thousands of years ago in the ancient Temple.

CREATE A COVER

The ḥallah we eat on Shabbat is usually covered with a decorated cloth. When we are ready to eat the ḥallah, we remove the cloth and everyone takes a piece of the bread. Decorate this ḥallah cover by tracing the design on the cloth below and then adding your own decorations. Can you read the Hebrew words you've made?

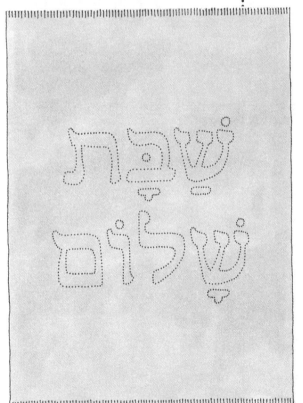

We cover the ḥallah with a cloth. The knife used to cut the ḥallah is also covered because a knife can be used as a weapon and Shabbat is a day of peace. Some people don't even use a knife. Instead they tear the bread with their hands.

We say a blessing, **hamotzi**, to thank God for the bread and all the food that we will eat at the meal.

בָּרוּךְ אַתָּה יְיָ אֱלֹהֵינוּ מֶלֶךְ הָעוֹלָם הַמּוֹצִיא לֶחֶם מִן הָאָרֶץ.

Blessed are You, Adonai our God, Ruler of the world, who brings forth bread from the earth.

Then we cut or tear the ḥallah and give a piece to each person. Put some salt on it. The salt adds a little extra taste in honor of Shabbat. It also reminds us of the salt used on the offerings in the ancient Temple.

After the meal we recite the Grace After Meals, **Birkat Hamazon**, and sing happy Shabbat songs.

IN THE SYNAGOGUE

On Friday evening there is a service in the synagogue. We sing **L'cha Dodi.** The song compares Shabbat to a beautiful queen. Some synagogues have family services.

Afterwards there may be an **Oneg Shabbat**, a celebration with tea,

In this synagogue young children have their very own service on Shabbat. The rabbi teaches them a lesson and together they sing Hebrew songs.

A PEACEFUL WEEK

What is your idea of spending a peaceful Shabbat with your family?

_____

_____

_____

_____

_____

_____

_____

coffee, and cake. It is a time for people to share family stories and talk about things that happened during the week.

On Shabbat morning we gather together for a service in the synagogue. The Torah is read and Sabbath prayers are recited. After the service there may be a Kiddush with wine, ḥallah, gefilte fish, and salty herring. People greet one another and say, "Shabbat Shalom" (שַׁבָּת שָׁלוֹם).

SHABBAT AFTERNOON

Shabbat is a time of peace, of **shalom** (שָׁלוֹם). During the week we are all busy. Children go to school. Parents work. But Shabbat is different. It is a time for rest, for reading, for spending time with friends and family. We do things to help us enjoy the wonderful world God has created. Each family has its own way of observing Shabbat.

HAVDALAH

We say good-bye to Shabbat with a prayer called **Havdalah** (הַבְדָּלָה). Havdalah means "separation"—it separates Shabbat from the new week that is beginning.

Some Jews look for three stars in the night sky before saying Havdalah. We light the tall, twisted Havdalah candle. The candle has many wicks

so the flame burns brightly. We hold a cup of wine and a box filled with sweet-smelling spices. Each person sniffs the spice box. We say good-bye to Shabbat hoping that its sweetness will last all week long. Just as we began Shabbat with wine, we end the holiday by sipping the sweet wine.

There is a legend that Elijah the prophet will bring peace to the world. During Havdalah we sing a song about him, **Eliyahu Hanavi**, because we hope that the peace of Shabbat will remain in the world every day of the year. And we wish one another "Shavuah Tov," a good week.

Shabbat is a gift from God. It is the gift of one special day in the week, every week of the year.

As we say good-bye to Shabbat we sniff the sweet-smelling spices in the Havdalah box. We hope that the sweetness of Shabbat will last all week long.

MY HOLIDAY DICTIONARY

BIRKAT HAMAZON Grace After Meals, the prayer we recite after we eat a meal

ELIYAHU HANAVI a song about Elijah the Prophet that we sing during the Havdalah service

ḤALLAH a braided bread made with eggs and white flour

HAMOTZI the blessing we recite before we eat bread

HAVDALAH the Hebrew word for "separation"—it is the prayer we recite on Saturday evening to say good-bye to Shabbat

KIDDUSH the prayer we recite with wine which tells everyone that Shabbat is a holy day.

L'CHA DODI a song we sing on Shabbat that compares Shabbat to a beautiful queen

ONEG SHABBAT a celebration after the Friday evening service

SHALOM the Hebrew word for peace

Tishre תִּשְׁרֵי

Ḥeshvan חֶשְׁוָן

Kislev  כִּסְלֵו

Tevet טֵבֵת

Shevat שְׁבָט

Adar אֲדָר

Nisan נִיסָן

Iyar אִיָּר

Sivan סִיוָן

Tammuz תַּמּוּז

Av אָב

Elul אֱלוּל

*And so they kept
the dedication of the
altar eight days.*

I MACCABEES 4:59

Did you ever lose
something that was
important to you?
Remember how good you
felt when you got it back?

Once, something was
taken from the Jewish
people.

This is what happened.

ḤANUKKAH

חֲנֻכָּה

WHY WE CELEBRATE

THE ḤANUKKAH STORY

Long, long ago, the Jewish people prayed in the Temple in Jerusalem. Jews came from all over the land of Israel to worship there. They celebrated the Sabbath and festivals with old and new friends, and they offered sacrifices to God there.

At that time, over 2,000 years ago, the land of Israel was ruled by the Syrians. The Syrians followed Greek ways. They dressed in Greek robes, they spoke the Greek language, they read Greek books, and they played Greek games.

Long before your synagogue or your grandparents' synagogue was built, there was only one place where the Jewish People worshipped: the Temple in Jerusalem.

We aren't certain what the first Temple looked like. This is a model of the second Temple.

Many Jews also followed Greek ways. But there was one thing the Jews would not do. They would not worship the Greek gods. No matter what the Jews looked like on the outside, on the inside they remained faithful to God.

The ruler of the Syrians was a king named **Antiochus**.

Antiochus commanded: The Jews may no longer study Torah. They may not celebrate Jewish holy days and festivals. And they may not observe Shabbat. All the Jews of Israel must worship Greek gods. Anyone who does not obey my order will be put to death.

COMPLETE THE PICTURE

Connect the dots to see the Temple in Jerusalem.

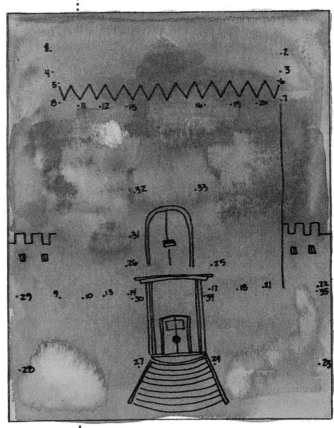

WHAT IS IT?

What does the word "Maccabee" mean? Color in each box with a dot in it. When you are finished you will see a picture of what the word "Maccabee" means. Write the name of the object beneath the picture.

MACCABEE MEANS

_____

Why do you think Judah's soldiers were called the Maccabees?

The wicked king and his soldiers put Greek idols in the Temple.
They tore down the stone altar.
They put out the **Eternal Light**.
They took our Temple away from us.

In a small town, not far from Jerusalem, there lived a Jewish priest named **Mattathias**. Mattathias was a brave man. He had faith in God. And he was not afraid of the Syrians.

"I will not bow down to the Greek idols," declared Mattathias. "All who are for God, follow me!"

Mattathias and his five sons hid in the mountains. Other Jews joined them and they soon had a small army. One of Mattathias' sons, **Judah**, was their leader. Judah and his army became known as the **Maccabees**.

Antiochus had a huge army with thousands and thousands of soldiers. Some rode on elephants so large that the earth shook when they marched. The Syrians laughed at Judah and his tiny army. The Syrians thought that no one could defeat them.

But Judah and the Maccabees knew the land well. They knew the best places to hide and the best places to fight. They moved fast among the rocks and over the hills. Their faith in God made them brave.

BE A MACCABEE

Judah and the Maccabees fought for something they believed in. Being able to pray, to celebrate, to study, and to live as a Jew was something that Judah would not allow any king or army to take away.

Below is a picture of Judah carrying a blank banner. Fill in the banner with the words that tell how Judah felt when he and the army of Israel defeated the Syrians. (And while you're at it, color in Judah to help his picture come to life.)

For three long years the small group of courageous Jews fought the huge Syrian army. Finally, the Maccabees drove Antiochus' soldiers out of Jerusalem. At last the Jews took back the Temple.

THE LEGEND OF THE OIL

Imagine how happy the Jews were to have the Temple back! But they had lots of work to do.

They destroyed the Greek idols. They cleaned the Temple from floor to ceiling. They rebuilt the altar. And they re-lit the Eternal Light. The Eternal Light was an oil lamp that burned in the Temple night and day.

Today, an Eternal Light burns in the synagogue. It reminds us that God is always with us.

78

There is a legend that when Judah entered the Temple to light the Eternal Light, he found only one jar of oil. It was enough to burn for just one day. But when Judah lit the lamp, the oil burned brightly for eight days!

From all over Israel the Jewish people came to the Temple. They brought offerings and sang songs of thanks to God.

This celebration was called Ḥanukkah, which means "dedication." The Jewish people rejoiced that they could worship God once again in the Temple.

JUDAH AND THE MACCABEES FIGHT AND DEFEAT ANTIOCHUS' ARMY

ANTIOCHUS FORBIDS THE JEWS TO WORSHIP GOD

THE JEWS ARE RULED BY THE SYRIANS

THE JEWS CLEAN THE TEMPLE AND CELEBRATE THE VICTORY

THE SYRIANS PUT GREEK IDOLS IN THE TEMPLE

WHAT HAPPENS NEXT?

Can you put the events of Ḥanukkah in the correct order? Each puzzle piece above contains one part of the Ḥanukkah story, but the pieces are mixed up. Write the number of each event in the circle so that they will tell the story of Ḥanukkah.

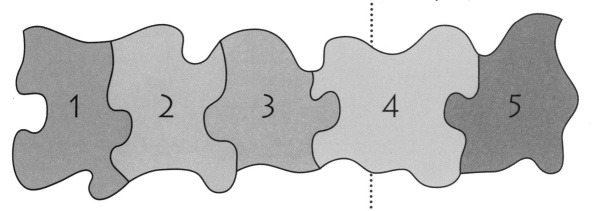

1   2   3   4   5

HOW WE CELEBRATE

THE FESTIVAL OF LIGHTS

We were so happy to have our Temple back that we have been celebrating Ḥanukkah ever since. And we were so happy that we could re-light the Eternal Light that today we light candles to celebrate Ḥanukkah. We use a special menorah called a **ḥanukkiah.**

A Ḥanukkah menorah comes in many shapes and sizes. It can be made of clay or wood or brass, but every ḥanukkiah holds nine candles.

To light the ḥanukkiah, place the **shamash** candle in its special holder. The shamash is the candle that is used to light all the others. The name shamash means "helper."

As you face the ḥanukkiah, place the first candle on your right. On each night add one more candle. On the first night there will be the shamash and one candle. On the second night there will be the shamash and two candles. The shamash always lights the newest candle first.

During the winter the sun sets early. The nights are dark and long. When we light the Ḥanukkah candles, we see beautiful, bright lights. We feel warm and safe. Look into the flames. Some say the lights can help us to see the miracle of the Maccabees all over again.

LIGHTING THE CANDLES

In the menorahs below, draw in the correct number of candles for the different nights of Ḥanukkah.

The third night of Ḥanukkah

The fifth night of Ḥanukkah

The seventh night of Ḥanukkah

Say the blessings before you light the candles:

בָּרוּךְ אַתָּה יְיָ
אֱלֹהֵינוּ מֶלֶךְ הָעוֹלָם
אֲשֶׁר קִדְּשָׁנוּ בְּמִצְוֹתָיו וְצִוָּנוּ
לְהַדְלִיק נֵר שֶׁל חֲנֻכָּה.

Blessed are You, Adonai our God, Ruler of the world, who makes us holy with mitzvot, and commands us to kindle the Ḥanukkah lights.

בָּרוּךְ אַתָּה יְיָ
אֱלֹהֵינוּ מֶלֶךְ הָעוֹלָם
שֶׁעָשָׂה נִסִּים לַאֲבוֹתֵינוּ
בַּיָּמִים הָהֵם בַּזְּמַן הַזֶּה.

Blessed are You, Adonai our God, Ruler of the world, who did wondrous things for our people long ago at this time of year.

On the first night of Ḥanukkah we also recite the Sheheḥeyanu blessing.

בָּרוּךְ אַתָּה יְיָ
אֱלֹהֵינוּ מֶלֶךְ הָעוֹלָם
שֶׁהֶחֱיָנוּ וְקִיְּמָנוּ וְהִגִּיעָנוּ
לַזְּמַן הַזֶּה.

Blessed are You, Adonai our God, Ruler of the world, who has given us life, sustained us, and brought us to this season of joy.

DREIDEL

There is a Ḥanukkah game that Jews have been playing for a very long time. Your parents, your grandparents, and even your great grandparents probably played it. It is called the **dreidel** game.

To play the dreidel game each player needs some candies or pennies. Each player puts one into the "pot." Everyone takes turns spinning the dreidel.

DID YOU WIN?

Write the name of the letter shown on each of the four dreidels. Beneath the name write what the letter tells you to do in the dreidel game.

If the dreidel falls on:

נ Nun = you don't take anything

ג Gimmel = you get to take everything in the "pot"

ה Hay = you take half the "pot"

ש Shin = you must put one back into the "pot."

The player with the most candies or pennies wins.

LATKES

Most Jewish holidays have a special food. Do you remember what sweet things we eat on Rosh Hashanah?

We eat apples dipped in honey. On Passover we eat matzah. But on Ḥanukkah we eat something hot and crispy. We eat potato pancakes called **latkes**.

To make latkes:
First we first grate the potatoes.
Then we add eggs, flour, and onion.

Next we mix them all together and fry the batter in hot oil. This reminds us of the oil used to light the Eternal Light in the Temple.

When the pancakes are brown and crispy, drain them on paper towels. Eat them with apple sauce or sour cream or both. Latkes are delicious. In Israel, people also eat doughnuts fried in oil. These are called *sufganiot*.

Write the number of each Ḥanukkah object next to its name.

☐ Ḥanukkiah ☐ Eternal Light
☐ Dreidel ☐ Latkes

ḤANUKKAH GELT

Everyone likes presents. On Ḥanukkah we give gifts to our families and to people who are important to us. Parents often give Ḥanukkah money—**gelt**—to children.

It is important not only to get gifts but to give them as well. Maybe you can

celebrate the holiday by giving some of your gelt to the poor. In this way you can help those who need it most.

Ḥanukkah is a time for celebration. For eight days we celebrate the victory of the Maccabees.

For eight days we celebrate the time when our ancestors took back the Temple.

For eight days we celebrate the first time in history that a people fought to keep their religion.

And for eight days we remember how to make the lights of Jewish living shine brightly in our homes and in our lives.

MY HOLIDAY DICTIONARY

ANTIOCHUS wicked ruler over Israel who tried to make the Jews worship Greek gods

DREIDEL four-sided top used in the Ḥanukkah game

ETERNAL LIGHT oil lamp in the Temple that burned night and day

GELT Ḥanukkah money

ḤANUKKIAH a menorah that holds nine candles

JUDAH leader of the Maccabees who helped defeat Antiochus

LATKES crispy potato pancakes

MACCABEES the group of Jews who defeated Antiochus and his army—the word "Maccabee" means "hammer"

MATTATHIAS Jewish priest who would not obey Antiochus

NES GADOL HAYAH SHAM "A great wonder happened there"—the first letter of each Hebrew word appears on the dreidel

SHAMASH the "helper" candle used to light all the other candles in the ḥanukkiah

Tishre תִּשְׁרֵי

Ḥeshvan חֶשְׁוָן

Kislev כִּסְלֵו

Tevet טֵבֵת

Shevat  שְׁבָט

Adar אֲדָר

Nisan נִיסָן

Iyar אִיָּר

Sivan סִיוָן

Tammuz תַּמּוּז

Av אָב

Elul אֱלוּל

As the days of a tree,
so shall be the days
of My People.

ISAIAH 65:22

Have you ever planted a tree?
Did you plant it in your backyard?
This girl is planting a tree in Israel.
Did you know that you can plant
a tree in Israel too—without even
being there?

ט"ו בִּשְׁבָט

B'SHEVAT

Besides being useful, trees are very beautiful. Some are tall and green with long thin leaves. Some have round leaves shaped like hearts. And some have beautiful ruffled pink and white flowers. Trees can also be fun to climb.

WHY CELEBRATE TREES?

Trees are important to us in many ways. They give us delicious fruit to eat, like apples, pears, and peaches. Trees give us wood to build things, like houses, tables, and chairs. And their branches are homes to birds and animals.

Because trees are so important to us, we have a holiday for their birthday. We call it Tu B'Shevat.

A BIRTHDAY FOR TREES

It is important to know the birthday of trees because of a commandment in the Torah:

"For the first three years of a tree's life, you may not eat its fruit. During the fourth year, its fruit must be given to God. Only when a tree is five years old may you eat its fruit."

To observe this commandment, we must know how old a tree is. But it is not always easy to keep track of a tree's age. In fact, it is almost impossible to know the exact day when a tree becomes a year older. So, long ago the rabbis chose one special day. They chose the fifteenth day of the Hebrew month **Shevat**–Tu B'Shevat–to be the birthday for all trees.

Shevat was a good month to choose. In the Land of Israel, the months

WHERE DOES IT COME FROM?

Many things that we use are made from trees. On the tree below, find and circle all the objects that are made from trees.

LETTERS THAT COUNT

Each letter of the Hebrew alphabet stands for a number.

א = 1   ו = 6
ב = 2   ז = 7
ג = 3   ח = 8
ד = 4   ט = 9
ה = 5   And so on...

Use your math skills to figure out how the holiday of Tu B'Shevat got its name.

What number is ט _____ ?

What number is ו _____ ?

Now add up the two letters:

ט + ו = _____

Tu B'Shevat falls on the _____ day of the month Shevat.

When the letters ט and ו are put together—ט"ו—they make the sound Tu.

And that is how this holiday got its name: ט"ו בִּשְׁבָט

---

before Shevat are wet and rainy. But just as Shevat begins, the land warms up, and the first buds appear on the trees. It is a time for growth and life.

The Hebrew month of Shevat comes in late January or February, so it may still be cold outside where you live. The trees are just beginning to wake up from their winter rest. You may not see any buds yet, but in a few weeks they will begin to appear. Then they will open into green leaves. Some trees will have beautiful flowers. Later they will give us sweet fruit to eat.

TREES IN ISRAEL

Why do we plant trees on Tu B'Shevat?

About two thousand years ago, the Jewish People were forced to leave Israel. Other people ruled the land, but they did not take good care of it. After hundreds of years of wandering and living in many other places, our people

came home. Israel became a Jewish State in 1948.

The Jews who returned to Israel found the land in bad condition. Few trees still grew. Dry sand, rocks, and muddy swamps covered the ground.

So the Jews planted trees in the dry desert to make the land green again. They planted trees on rocky hills to make the soil rich and fertile. And

Imagine these hills without any trees. The **Jewish National Fund** (J.N.F.) has planted over 200 million trees in the Land of Israel.

they planted eucalyptus trees in the swamps to soak up the water.

Jews from all over the world gave money to plant trees in Israel, to make the Jewish State green and strong once more.

WHEN TO PLANT?

You can plant a tree in Israel at any time, but there are some special occasions when we plant trees to give thanks and to remember—when a baby is born, when a friend becomes a Bar or Bat Mitzvah, when someone gets married, when a close friend or relative dies.

TREES IN ISRAEL

By adding trees and coloring them, you can help turn this sandy and rocky picture into a green and beautiful one.

And when you plant a tree in Israel, you are also planting for our people's future.

Today, wherever you go in Israel you can see green forests and orchards filled with flowering fruit trees.

A TU B'SHEVAT SEDER

We are so happy that God created wonderful trees that we have a special celebration just for them. It's called a **Tu B'Shevat seder** (like a Passover seder).

We eat fruit that grows on trees in Israel and sing happy songs. We drink four different kinds of wine – dark red, light red, pink, and white.

BLESSING FOR FRUIT AND WINE

Not all fruit are alike. (Think how different watermelons and bananas are!) So on Tu B'Shevat we eat fruit in certain groupings:

This blue box is a special *tzedakah* box created by the Jewish National Fund (J.N.F.). We put money in these boxes. When they are full, we send the money to the J.N.F. The money is used to plant trees in Israel. The J.N.F. has been planting trees for over 90 years. So when we give money to the J.N.F. we are planting for Israel's future!

95

TRUE OR FALSE

Fill in the **T** if the sentence is true.
Fill in the **F** if the sentence is false.

1. Tu B'Shevat celebrates the birthday of trees.   T   F

2. The J.N.F. helps plant trees in Israel.   T   F

3. Trees are often planted when someone is born.   T   F

4. We celebrate Tu B'Shevat in the month of Adar.   T   F

One of the ways we take care of our world is by recycling paper. We collect newspapers for recycling. The recycling plant uses them to make new paper.

We eat oranges, grapefruits, and almonds – they have coverings on the outside. We eat dates and peaches, plums and olives – they have pits on the inside. And we eat raisins and figs – you can eat all of them, inside and outside.

At the Tu B'Shevat seder we say prayers to thank God. A story tells us why we say the blessings.

Once a man came to his friend's house. The man was about to eat without saying a blessing. His friend said to him, "Before you could have food to eat, God created a beautiful world filled with good soil, with seeds, and with sun and rain to make the plants grow." Then the man knew that he should thank God for his food, and he said a blessing.

PLANTING PARTNERS

God makes the seeds, the soil, the sun, and the rain, all of which make trees grow. But when you plant a seed you become God's partner.

One day an old woman was planting a fruit tree. People watched and laughed, "Old woman, why are you planting this tree? It will be many years before this tree gives fruit. You will not live long enough to see it."

The old woman answered, "When I was a little girl, I ate fruit because someone else planted trees before I was born. Now I plant trees. I will plant the seeds that God has made. God will make the sun shine and make the rain to water them. Years from now, after I am gone, my grandchildren will eat the fruit of this tree and sit in its shade on warm summer days."

When it is warm enough where you live, you may want to plant trees too.

PLANTING PARTNERS PLEDGE:

I hereby promise to care for our world and to keep it clean.

_____

I will plant _____

I will help my family to recycle

_____

_____

I will make Israel green and strong by

_____

_____

I will clean up our

_____

And to remember the lesson of Tu B'Shevat all year long, whenever I eat a fruit or vegetable, I will think about

_____

_____

Respectfully signed,

_____
OFFICIAL WORLD CARE-TAKER

TAKING CARE OF GOD'S WORLD

If you have a dog or a cat or a fish, you know that you have to take care of your pet. But we have to take care of our world too.

When God made the world, God said to Adam and Eve: I created my beautiful world for you to enjoy. Take very good care of it. Keep it clean, and make sure the plants are watered and the animals get fed. Do not destroy this beautiful world. It is the only one you have. You are its caretakers.

On Tu B'Shevat we thank God for the gifts of the earth and we remember our responsibility to continue to care for this wonderful world.

MY HOLIDAY DICTIONARY

JEWISH NATIONAL FUND the J.N.F. raises money to help improve the land of Israel

SHEVAT the fifth month of the Jewish year

TU B'SHEVAT the fifteenth day of the Hebrew month Shevat—on this day every tree becomes one year older

TU B'SHEVAT SEDER a ceremony to celebrate the New Year of the Trees—we sing songs, recite blessings, and eat the fruits and vegetables which grow in Israel

Tishre תִּשְׁרֵי

Ḥeshvan חֶשְׁוָן

Kislev כִּסְלֵו

Tevet טֵבֵת

Shevat שְׁבָט

Adar  אֲדָר

Nisan נִיסָן

Iyar אִיָּר

Sivan סִיוָן

Tammuz תַּמּוּז

Av אָב

Elul אֱלוּל

Purim is a special celebration, with carnivals and costumes, games and giggles.

We'll go to the synagogue and hear the story of brave Queen Esther, courageous Mordecai, and wicked Haman.

Make sure to bring your gragger. That's a noisemaker. You'll twirl it to drown out Haman's name.

And don't forget to dress up in your favorite costume. You can be anything from a king to a clown. But first, let's read the story of Purim.

Make them days of feasting and gladness, and of sending portions one to another, and gifts to the poor. **MEGILLAT ESTHER 9:22**

פּוּרִים

PURIM

WHY WE CELEBRATE

THE PURIM STORY

Long ago in the land of Persia there lived a king named **Ahasuerus**. The king lived in a great palace in the city of Shushan. His queen was the young and beautiful **Esther**. King Ahasuerus had chosen Esther from all the women in the land.

But there was one thing King Ahasuerus did not know about Esther. He did not know that Esther was Jewish.

Queen Esther had a cousin who loved her very much. His name was **Mordecai**. One day Mordecai heard two palace guards secretly planning to kill the king. Mordecai immediately went to Esther so that she could warn Ahasuerus.

The guards were arrested, King Ahasuerus was saved, and Mordecai's brave deed was recorded in the royal records.

Now, the king had an advisor. He was a wicked man named **Haman.**

A PAGE FROM THE PALACE RECORDS

Help record Mordecai's brave act. Using the words below, fill in the blanks to complete the palace records.

Let it be known that

_____

saved the life of King

_____.

Mordecai overheard a

_____

to kill the king. He told Queen

_____

who then reported it to the king.

The land of

_____

is grateful to Mordecai for his act of

_____.

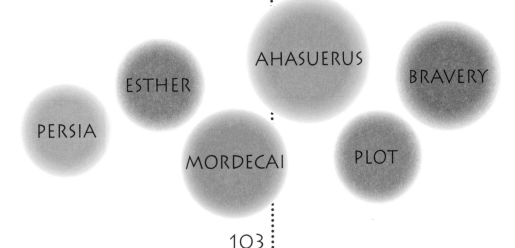

PERSIA
ESTHER
AHASUERUS
BRAVERY
MORDECAI
PLOT

MATCH THE HAT

Write the number of the hat next to the description of the person who wears it.

The king's wicked advisor_____

Esther's cousin_____

The beautiful queen of Persia_____

The king of Persia_____

Everywhere Haman went, he ordered people to bow down before him. And everyone obeyed.

But there was one man who refused to bow down to Haman. That man was Mordecai. Mordecai said, "I am a Jew and we bow only before God."

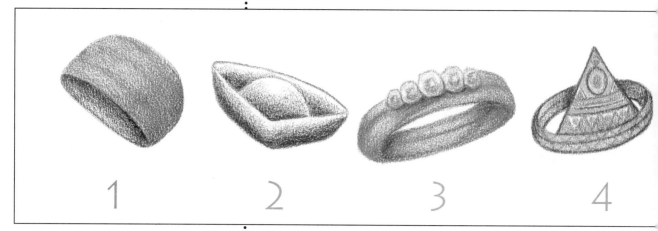

1   2   3   4

Haman was very angry. "Mordecai must die!" thought Haman. But Haman decided that killing Mordecai was not enough. Haman wanted to kill every Jew in the land of Persia.

So Haman brought his terrible plan to the king. He told King Ahasuerus,

"There is a group of people in our land who have different customs from ours. They refuse to obey the king's laws. Let us kill them and be rid of them forever."

Without thinking, the king agreed.

Haman was very pleased with his plan. He went home and rolled dice or lots (called **purim**) to help him choose the day to kill the Jews. The dice landed on the 13th day of the month **Adar**. On that day every Jew in Persia would die.

When Mordecai heard about Haman's plot, he sent word to Queen Esther, "You must speak to the king at once! You must convince him to take back this wicked order."

Esther replied, "But cousin Mordecai, no one can go before the king without being invited. I might be killed for doing that."

DIFFERENCES ARE DELIGHTFUL

Haman wanted to kill the Jewish people because they were different. But imagine how boring life might be if everyone looked, talked, and acted the same way.

Name three things that make you different from all your friends. Think of things that you like to do, music you like to play, sports you are good at.

1 _____

_____

2 _____

_____

3 _____

_____

Name three things that make your family special—different from other families.

1 _____

_____

2 _____

_____

3 _____

_____

Now compare your answers with those of your friends to see how important, and how much fun, understanding our differences can be.

Fill in the **T** if the sentence is true.
Fill in the **F** if the sentence is false.

1. King Ahasuerus knew that Queen Esther was Jewish. T F

2. Mordecai saved the king's life. T F

3. Mordecai would not bow down before Haman. T F

4. Haman wanted to help the Jews. T F

5. Mordecai believed that Jews bow down only before God. T F

But Mordecai urged her. He explained, "Only you, Esther, can save the Jewish people!"

Esther thought long and hard. Finally she decided, "I cannot let my people die. No one can destroy us for being different. Tonight I will go before the king. And if I perish, I perish."

Esther was very frightened! Would the king refuse to see her? The young queen gathered all her courage and strength and went before the king. As she approached King Ahasuerus, he held out his golden scepter and said, "Whatever you ask, Esther, it shall be done."

Esther told the king, "There is a man who wishes to kill my people, the Jewish people. I am Jewish and he wants to kill me too."

"Who is the man who would do such a terrible thing?" demanded King Ahasuerus.

"It is your advisor, Haman. I beg you to stop him!" she cried.

King Ahasuerus was angrier than angry. He was furious! He said, "I will not let Haman harm you or your people. Haman will be killed for his evil plot.

And your cousin Mordecai shall be my new advisor."

And so it was. On the 14th day of the month of Adar, the Jews of Shushan celebrated and rejoiced because they were saved from destruction. They sent gifts of gladness to one another, and gave food to feed the poor.

And they called the holiday "Purim" because Haman used purim, dice, to decide when to kill the Jewish people.

Today, we still celebrate Purim joyfully on the 14th of Adar. Remembering the bravery of Esther and Mordecai, we give thanks that our people were saved in Shushan long ago.

MYSTERY WORDS

Cross out the letters in each line that appear three times. Use the remaining letters to complete the sentence below.

J B M R A M V J E R J Y M

C O L U H R L H A H G L E

X X L O S Y Q A L Q T S X Q S Y

By risking her life, Esther showed her

_____, _____,

and her_____

to the Jewish People.

HOW WE CELEBRATE

THE MEGILLAH READING

On Purim we go to the synagogue and listen as the story of Esther is read out loud. The story is written on a scroll called a **megillah**.

ויהי בימי אחשורוש הוא אחשורוש המלך
מהדו ועד כוש שבע ועשרים ומאה מדינה
בימים ההם כשבת המלך אחשורוש על כסא
מלכותו אשר בשושן הבירה בשנת שלוש
למלכו עשה משתה לכל שריו ועבדיו חיל פרס
ומדי הפרתמים ושרי המדינות לפניו בהראתו את
עשר כבוד מלכותו ואת יקר תפארת גדולתו ימים
רבים שמונים ומאת יום ובמלואת הימים האלה
עשה המלך לכל העם הנמצאים בשושן הבירה
למגדול ועד קטן משתה שבעת ימים בחצר
גנת ביתן המלך חור כרפס ותכלת אחוז בחבלי
בוץ וארגמן על גלילי כסף ועמודי שש מטות זהב
וכסף על רצפת בהט ושש ודר וסחרת והשקות
בכלי זהב וכלים מכלים שונים ויין מלכות רב כיד

Whenever we hear Haman's name we stamp our feet and twirl our noisemakers round and round. We drown out Haman's name with our **graggers**.

We try to yell and boo so loud that no one will even hear his evil name.

Twirling the graggers reminds us that it is our duty to "stamp out" hatred whenever we see or hear it. It is our responsibility to drown out the evil voices who tell us to treat people unfairly just because they are different.

Some graggers are made of wood. Some are made of metal. All of them make a lot of noise.

Purim is a noisy, jolly holiday. We wear masks and dress up in colorful silly costumes.

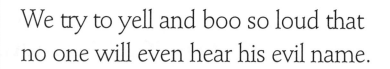

Pretending to be someone else on Purim can be lots of fun. You can be Esther or Mordecai. You can be a king, a queen, or even a wicked advisor.

HAMANTASHEN

After the megillah reading we'll eat **hamantashen**, sweet cakes filled with fruit or poppy seeds.

DESIGN YOUR OWN MASK

Will you be Haman, Mordecai, Esther, or Ahasuerus?

Draw the Purim character you want to be on this mask.

111

CHEF SHUSHAN

King Ahasuerus has asked you to prepare a new and different food to celebrate Purim. It must help remind people of the story in some way.

Draw your new food below, and don't forget to include the recipe!

Hamantashen are made in the shape of a triangle. They remind us of Haman's three-cornered hat.

In Hebrew, hamantashen are called *oznai Haman*, which actually means "Haman's ears." When we eat Purim cakes, we

remember not only Haman's hat, but his pointy ears as well!

Can you see the part of the word "hamantashen" that comes from the name Haman?

MISHLOAḤ MANOT

When Esther and Mordecai saved the Jews, everyone was very happy. The Jews of Shushan celebrated by sharing their happiness in a very Jewish way. They sent gifts to one another.

Today, we still follow this custom. It's called **mishloaḥ manot**—sending gifts. We can send baskets of fruit and cookies to friends and families. You can also show your thanks by sending

WRITE YOUR OWN MEGILLAH

Now that you know the Purim tale, why not write a Purim story of your own. Create a different sort of megillah by filling in the blanks with silly names, places, or any words that you want. Remember, making jokes is part of the Purim celebration.

_____, the king of Persia, married the beautiful Jewish woman named _____.

_____ refused to bow down before the king's chief advisor, named _____, who wanted to kill all the _____ in Persia. When Esther told the king about Haman's evil plot, the king ordered that Haman be _____. All the Jews of Persia were saved. We celebrate their victory on the holiday called

_____.

gifts to the poor. In that way you bring happiness to those who need it most.

The Purim story gives us courage. In times of trouble we must help one another.

The Purim story makes us strong. Esther's bravery teaches us that we can be brave too.

CAN YOU FIND IT?

Purim is a time when we wear disguises and dress up in costumes. We can often fool people by pretending to be someone else. Hidden in the picture above are five Purim objects. Can you find them?

Did you find the gragger, the megillah, the king's crown, a gift basket of food (mishloaḥ manot), and hamantashen?

And the Purim story makes us proud. You can be like Esther. You can be like Mordecai. Remember what they did to protect our people.

And when you feel proud to be Jewish, you can make our people strong and safe.

MY HOLIDAY DICTIONARY

ADAR on the thirteenth day of this Hebrew month the Jews of Persia were saved—on the fourteenth day we celebrate

AHASUERUS king of Persia

ESTHER the Jewish queen of Persia who risked her life to save her people

GRAGGER noisemakers we twirl whenever we hear Haman's name

HAMAN King Ahasuerus' evil advisor who wanted to kill the Jews

HAMANTASHEN sweet triangular cakes filled with fruit or poppy seeds—they remind us of Haman's three-cornered hat

MEGILLAH a scroll—in the synagogue we read aloud the story of Purim from the Scroll of Esther

MISHLOAH MANOT baskets of food or gifts we send to one another at Purim

MORDECAI Queen Esther's cousin who helped save the Jews of Persia

PURIM the word "purim" refers to the lots or dice Haman used to decide on which day to kill the Jews

Tishre תִּשְׁרֵי

Ḥeshvan חֶשְׁוָן

Kislev כִּסְלֵו

Tevet טֵבֵת

Shevat שְׁבָט

Adar אֲדָר

Nisan  נִיסָן

Iyar אִיָּר

Sivan סִיוָן

Tammuz תַּמּוּז

Av אָב

Elul אֱלוּל

All people, in every generation, must regard themselves as having been personally freed from Egypt. **HAGGADAH**

PASSOVER

פֶּסַח

You already know that we eat matzah on Passover. And you probably can't wait to search for the piece of matzah that is hidden. You may even get a prize for finding it. But did you know that one of the most important parts of the Passover holiday is you?

At the holiday meal a child asks four important questions.

To answer these four questions we tell an ancient story.

WHY WE CELEBRATE

THE PASSOVER STORY

Long, long ago our people lived in the land of Egypt. The ruler of Egypt was **Pharaoh**. Pharaoh was afraid that the People of Israel were becoming too strong. So he made them slaves.

Pharaoh forced our people to work in the hot sun. They pulled large heavy stones and made bricks from clay. They built great cities for Pharaoh. The work was hard and dangerous, and the Jewish slaves were not allowed to rest.

The cruel Egyptian masters often beat the slaves to make them work even harder. But Pharaoh was still afraid. He thought that our people were becoming too strong and too many. So Pharaoh ordered his servants to drown every Hebrew baby boy in the Nile River.

But one baby boy was saved. His name was **Moses**. His mother put him in a basket in the river, hoping that his life would be saved. An Egyptian princess found him floating down the Nile, and raised him as her very own son.

When Moses was a grown man, he saw a bush on fire in the desert. Moses looked closely at the bush, and he saw that it was not burned by the flames. Then, from the bush came the voice of God. God told Moses to free the People of Israel.

TRUE OR FALSE

Fill in the **T** if the sentence is true.
Fill in the **F** if the sentence is false.

1. The Jewish people once lived in Egypt.   T   F

2. When the Jews were slaves, their lives were easy.   T   F

3. Pharaoh was the ruler of Egypt.   T   F

4. The Egyptian masters were kind to the Hebrew slaves.   T   F

5. Pharaoh was afraid of the People of Israel.   T   F

LET'S PRETEND

Pretend you are Pharaoh's daughter. Suddenly, you notice a basket in the reeds. You go over to it and look inside.
Now tell what you are thinking.

Pretend you are Moses, raised in the palace of Pharaoh. You see your people suffering but you don't know what to do. One day you see an Egyptian beating a Hebrew slave.
You rush over and strike the Egyptian slave master. The Hebrew slave runs away unharmed.
Now tell what you are thinking.

Moses listened to God's voice. Then he went to Pharaoh and said, "Let my people go!"

But Pharaoh was stubborn. He said, "No."

So God tried to change Pharaoh's mind by making ten terrible things happen in the land of Egypt. We call them the **Ten Plagues**.

First the Nile river turned to blood. דָּם

Then frogs covered the land. צְפַרְדֵּעַ

Next flying bugs filled the air. כִּנִּים

Then God sent wild beasts. עָרוֹב

Soon all the cattle died. דֶּבֶר

Then the Egyptians were covered with sores. שְׁחִין

Next, sharp, icy hailstones fell from the sky. בָּרָד

Soon clouds of insects called locusts ate the crops. אַרְבֶּה

And then it became very, very dark. חֹשֶׁךְ

After each plague Moses would say, "Let my people go." And each time Pharaoh would answer, "No!" He would not free the People of Israel.

Then came the last and most terrible plague of all. "The first-born child of every Egyptian family will die," warned Moses. But Pharaoh did not listen. He would not let our people go free.

So the plague of death (מַכַּת בְּכוֹרוֹת) came to every city and village in the land of Egypt. Every first-born died, even Pharaoh's son. But God protected the children of the Hebrews. The tenth plague passed over their houses. And that is why we call this holiday Passover.

WORD SEARCH

Circle the name of each plague you find.

After you circle each plague write it on the lines below.

H	B	K	B	U	G	S	E
A	L	T	M	N	T	P	T
I	O	S	H	H	F	A	S
L	O	C	U	S	T	S	P
R	D	F	R	O	G	S	H
I	E	O	N	D	S	H	E

1 _____

2 _____

3 _____

4 _____

5 _____

Can you name the other five plagues?

6 _____

7 _____

8 _____

9 _____

10 _____

At last, Pharaoh said to Moses, "Go! Take your people from this land."

The People of Israel left Egypt in a great hurry. They were afraid that Pharaoh might change his mind. And he did.

"Bring the people back," ordered Pharaoh. "We need those slaves to do our work."

The Egyptian army chased after the Israelites. They followed them to the edge of a big sea. There was no way to escape.

But God sent a great wind. It pushed apart the waters of the sea. The Israelites crossed safely on dry land. And when the armies of Egypt followed after them, the waters returned and the Egyptian soldiers drowned in the sea.

After generations of living as slaves in Egypt, the People of Israel were free at last! They were free to worship God. And they were free to return to our homeland, the Land of Israel.

HOW WE CELEBRATE

Seder means "order." During the seder we eat, we tell the story of Passover, and we sing. We do this every year in the very same order.

THE SEDER

The Passover story is so important to us that we tell it every year. We want every person to feel as though he or she had actually gone out from Egypt.

We remember that we, too, were once slaves in the land of Egypt. On Passover, Pesaḥ, the whole family comes together for a wonderful feast called a **seder.**

At the seder we read the story of the Exodus out loud from a book called the **Haggadah**. Haggadah is the Hebrew word for "telling." By reading the Haggadah we relive the journey of our people from slavery in Egypt to freedom in the Promised Land.

THE FOUR QUESTIONS

One of the first things we do at the seder is to ask the four questions.

The children who read the questions are not only looking for an answer, but they are also showing the world that we are no longer slaves. Free people can ask questions. We can search for answers. And we are free to celebrate the festivals of the Jewish people.

CAN YOU LEARN TO ASK THE FOUR QUESTIONS?

Why is this night different from all nights?
Why do we eat only matzah tonight?

מַה נִּשְׁתַּנָּה הַלַּיְלָה הַזֶּה מִכָּל־הַלֵּילוֹת?
שֶׁבְּכָל־הַלֵּילוֹת אָנוּ אוֹכְלִין חָמֵץ וּמַצָּה.
הַלַּיְלָה הַזֶּה כֻּלּוֹ מַצָּה.

Why do we eat bitter herbs on Pesaḥ?

שֶׁבְּכָל־הַלֵּילוֹת אָנוּ אוֹכְלִין שְׁאָר יְרָקוֹת.
הַלַּיְלָה הַזֶּה מָרוֹר.

Why do we dip twice?

שֶׁבְּכָל־הַלֵּילוֹת אֵין אָנוּ מַטְבִּילִין אֲפִלּוּ פַּעַם אֶחָת.
הַלַּיְלָה הַזֶּה שְׁתֵּי פְעָמִים.

Why do we recline or lean back at the table?

שֶׁבְּכָל־הַלֵּילוֹת אָנוּ אוֹכְלִין בֵּין יוֹשְׁבִין וּבֵין מְסֻבִּין.
הַלַּיְלָה הַזֶּה כֻּלָּנוּ מְסֻבִּין.

125

FEEL FREE TO ASK

What questions would you like to ask at the seder?

Think about all the things we eat, the story we tell, and the things we do on Passover.

Now write four more questions you would like to ask.

1 _____
_____
_____ ?

2 _____
_____
_____ ?

3 _____
_____
_____ ?

4 _____
_____
_____ ?

WHY DO WE EAT MATZAH?

At the seder, and during the whole week of Passover, we eat **matzah** (מַצָּה). Matzah is flat, because there is no leavening in it. Leavening makes bread dough rise. Tradition tells us that the People of Israel were in such a hurry to leave Egypt, they did not wait for their bread to rise. They put it on their backs and the sun baked it into hard, flat bread. We eat matzah on Passover to taste the hardship of slavery.

The memories our people have of leaving Egypt are so important that during Passover we do not eat any bread or food which has leaven in it.

In Hebrew, leaven is called ḥametz. Before Passover we remove from our houses all bread or food that was made with ḥametz. And during the holiday we don't buy anything that has ḥametz in it.

INVITING GUESTS

One of the prayers in the Haggadah begins, "This is the bread of hardship... let anyone who is hungry come and eat...." The matzah reminds us to invite guests to the seder so that no one is alone on Passover. It also reminds us to give money to feed the hungry.

THE FOUR CUPS OF WINE

During the seder we drink four cups of wine. Each cup reminds us of one of the promises God made to Israel:

"I will free you from Egypt."
"I will deliver you from slavery."
"I will lead you home."
"You will be My people."

THE SEARCH FOR LEAVEN

Before Passover begins, we search every corner of the house to make sure we have no ḥametz, חָמֵץ. Help get this kitchen ready for Passover by putting an X on all the ḥametz you find.

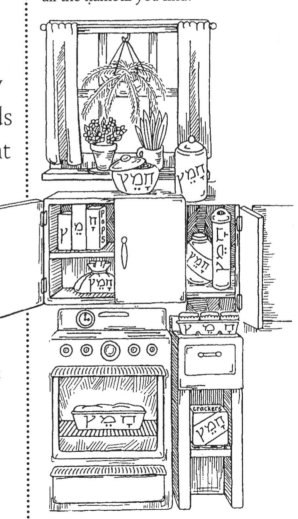

127

Jewish legend tells that when the People of Israel crossed the sea, the angels sang songs of joy to thank God for saving the Israelites.

But God silenced the angels, saying, "The Egyptians are drowning. You shouldn't shout out in joy!"

And so, today, when we celebrate the seder, we pour a few drops of wine from our cup. We do this because others had to lose their lives so that the People of Israel could gain its freedom.

What lesson does this story teach us?

If you were one of the joyful angels, how would you respond to God's statement?

As we say the blessing and drink each cup of wine, we remember God's promises and hope that God will free those Jews who are not free to live as Jews, and all people who do not have freedom. We also recall the promise we make to God: to live as Jews, to study Torah, and to work for freedom.

THE CUP OF ELIJAH

On the seder table is a cup of wine called the **Cup of Elijah**. It is reserved for a special guest, the prophet Elijah.

Jewish tradition teaches us about a special hope: One day, the story says, Elijah will return and bring a time of peace and freedom for everyone.

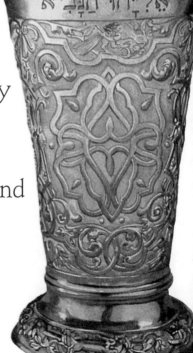

During the seder we open the door to invite Elijah to join us. Maybe someday, with your help, we can make that dream come true.

THE SEDER PLATE

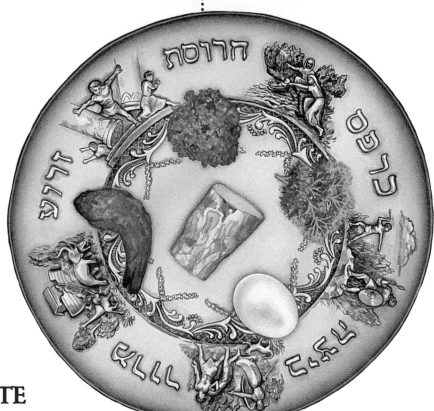

On the seder table is a plate with five foods on it—a lamb bone; a green herb (like parsley); bitter herbs (usually horseradish); a mixture of chopped nuts, apples, and wine called ḥaroset; and a roasted egg.

These are the symbols of Pesaḥ. These symbols help remind us of Passover's many messages.

The roasted lamb bone or *zeroah* reminds us of the spring sacrifices

A thing that helps us remember something else is called a symbol. On the seder plate above are five symbols of Passover.

129

that were offered in the Temple in Jerusalem.

The green herbs and the egg remind us of the new life that grows each spring. We dip the parsley in salt water to remind us of the tears our people cried when they were slaves in Egypt.

The bitter herbs, **maror,** remind us of the bitterness of slavery.

MAKE THE CONNECTIONS

Write the number of the picture next to the food it gives us for the seder plate.

EGG ____
LAMB BONE ____
ḤAROSET ____
PARSLEY ____
HORSERADISH ____

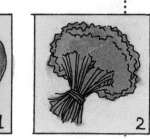
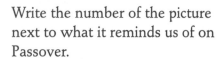

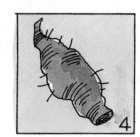

Write the number of the picture next to what it reminds us of on Passover.

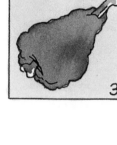
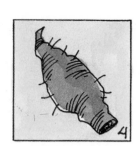

THE TEMPLE ____
SLAVERY ____
BRICKS ____
NEW LIFE ____
TEARS ____

And the haroset reminds us of the clay used to make bricks. During the seder we dip maror in the haroset and eat them together.

WHY DO WE RECLINE?

During the seder you can lean back or recline at the table because in ancient times free people relaxed when they ate. Some people have pillows to make them feel even more comfortable. Maybe you can make a special cushion of your own.

AFIKOMAN

Afikoman means "dessert." On the seder table there is a plate with three pieces of matzah. During the seder one small piece of matzah is hidden. This is the afikoman. You and the other children at the seder can look for it. The one who finds it will get a prize.

A PRECIOUS GIFT

Telling the Passover story is one of the most important mitzvot in Jewish life. Parents are commanded to tell this story to their children, and to their grandchildren. Every family tells and retells the tale,

AFIKOMAN BAG

The afikoman is often placed in a special bag before it is hidden. Decorate this bag to show a part of the Passover story.

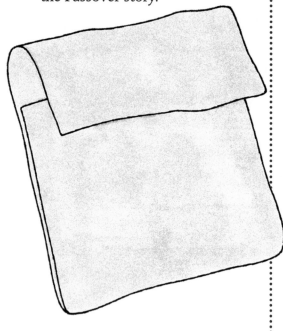

passing it on as a gift, a precious lesson.

The Exodus story is important because it reminds us we were once slaves in Egypt. So the Torah tells us we must be careful to treat other people with kindness and must work to free all people who are oppressed.

Passover is important because we remember that God brought us out of Egypt. It gives us hope that God will end all oppression in the world.

When you are at your family seder, think of the other Jewish children around the world. They are doing the same things you are doing, on this very same night. They read the Haggadah that you read. They drink wine and eat matzah. They thank God for their freedom, just as you do. And like you, they give thanks for the new life that comes each spring.

MY HOLIDAY DICTIONARY

AFIKOMAN the piece of matzah we look for at the end of the seder

CUP OF ELIJAH the cup of wine that is set on the seder table for the prophet Elijah

FOUR QUESTIONS usually read by the youngest child, these questions are answered by telling the story of Passover

HAGGADAH the Hebrew word for "telling"—we read aloud from this book each year at the Passover seder to relive the journey of our people from slavery to freedom

HAMETZ the Hebrew word for leaven—ḥametz makes bread rise, so during Passover we do not eat food made with ḥametz

HAROSET a mixture of chopped nuts, apples, and wine which reminds us of the clay that the Jewish slaves used to make bricks

MAROR the bitter herbs which remind us of the bitterness of slavery

MATZAH the flat bread we eat during the week of Passover to remind us of our ancestors' quick flight from Egypt

MOSES led the Jews out of slavery in Egypt

PHARAOH the ruler of Egypt who was afraid that the Jews were becoming too strong so he made them slaves

SEDER the Hebrew word for "order"—the Passover feast at which we tell the story of Passover, eat, and sing songs, always in the same order

TEN PLAGUES the terrible events which happened in Egypt when Pharaoh refused to free the Jewish people

YOM HASHOAH

יוֹם הַשּׁוֹאָה

Nisan 27 נִיסָן

Most of our holidays are happy. They help us to remember great and wonderful things, like a queen saving our people in Persia.

Some holidays are very sad. They remind us of things too important to forget.

Not very long ago, a most terrible disaster happened to

our people. Your grandparents probably remember it. A very evil man came to power in Germany. He was like Haman, who had wanted to kill all the Jews. But this time there was no brave queen like Esther to stop his terrible plan. Six million Jews were murdered.

We try to remember every one of them. We think about them all through the year, but we especially remember them on Holocaust Memorial Day, Yom Hashoah.

Many communities hold prayer services on this sad day. Yahrzeit memorial candles are lit in memory of the children, parents, and grandparents who were killed. We recite the mourner's prayer, the *Kaddish*.

On Yom Hashoah we remind ourselves that some people can be terribly cruel. We remind ourselves that some people can be very brave when they try to help others. We must never forget. Remembering will help us prevent such a terrible thing from ever happening again.

Tishre	תִּשְׁרֵי
Ḥeshvan	חֶשְׁוָן
Kislev	כִּסְלֵו
Tevet	טֵבֵת
Shevat	שְׁבָט
Adar	אֲדָר
Nisan	נִיסָן
Iyar	אִיָּר 
Sivan	סִיוָן
Tammuz	תַּמּוּז
Av	אָב
Elul	אֱלוּל

There are lots of birthdays in the Jewish year. In the fall we celebrate the birthday of the world, Rosh Hashanah. In the winter we enjoy the birthday for trees, Tu B'Shevat. And in the spring we celebrate Yom Ha'atzma'ut, the birthday of the State of Israel.

YOM

יוֹם הָעַצְמָאוּת

HA'ATZMA'UT

The hope of two thousand years.

HATIKVAH

Jews in Israel celebrate the birthday of Israel with colorful parades, music, dancing, and food.

ISRAEL'S BIRTHDAY

Israel's birthday comes on the fifth day of the Hebrew month Iyar. That Hebrew date is usually in the month of May. It was on this day, in 1948, that Israel became a nation, a homeland for Jews around the world. It is a happy day in the Land of Israel and for Jews everywhere.

NEVER FORGETTING ISRAEL

Long ago, our people had our own country—Israel (יִשְׂרָאֵל). We lived there for a thousand years.

During that time, great kings like David and Solomon ruled the land. Prophets like Amos and Isaiah reminded us to be kind and fair. Great rabbis taught us to love one another.

Then, about two thousand years ago, our land was ruled by foreign countries. The Temple in Jerusalem was destroyed. We were forced to leave our homes in Israel.

WHERE DID WE GO?

Jews live all over the world. Below are six countries. Unscramble the letters of each country to discover some of the places where Jews live.

Jewish people were scattered across the world. We stopped speaking Hebrew and began to learn the languages of the countries where we lived. We spoke French, Russian, Spanish, Arabic, and English. Hebrew was used only when praying, or for studying our sacred books.

But our people did not forget the Land of Israel. Every year at the Passover seder we would say, "Next Year in Jerusalem!"

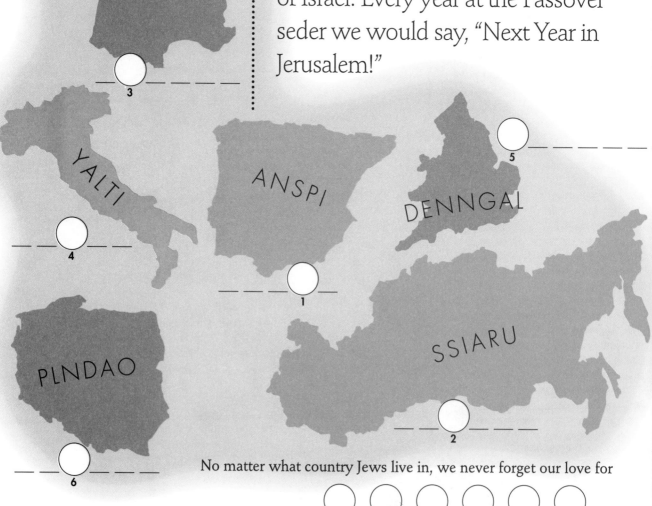

CEFRAN

_ _O_ _ _ _ _
  3

YALTI

_ _O_ _ _
 4

ANSPI

_ _ _ _O_
    1

DENNGAL

O_ _ _ _ _ _
5

SSIARU

_ _ _O_ _ _
   2

PLNDAO

_ _O_ _ _
  6

No matter what country Jews live in, we never forget our love for

O O O O O O
1 2 3 4 5 6

140

This boy is playing on a tractor. Years ago it was used to farm the land. Now the tractor is part of a playground in a kibbutz, a small community in Israel where people work and live together.

We spoke of our love for Israel in our prayers. We even faced Jerusalem when we prayed. Our people longed to have our own country once again.

RETURNING TO THE LAND

About 100 years ago, a small group of Russian Jews decided it was time to move back to Israel. At about that same time, a man named **Theodor Herzl** was urging Jews around the world to rebuild Israel. The Jews deserve a land of their own, Herzl said. The belief that Jews should have their own country is called **Zionism**.

Jews began to return to Israel. When Jews move to Israel it is called making **aliyah**. The Jewish people wanted a country of their own, one that would be a Jewish state. But they had much work to do.

They drained the muddy swamps and learned to farm the land. They grew fruits and vegetables, even in the dry desert sand. They built houses, schools, and roads.

PEN PAL

Write a letter to a friend in Israel. What questions would you like to ask? What would you like to tell your Israeli friend about life in America? What do you think might be similar about your lives? What might be different?

Dear_____,

_____

_____

_____

_____

_____

_____

_____

_____

_____

_____

Your Pen Pal,

_____

INDEPENDENCE

But Israel was still under foreign rule. Finally, in 1947, the United Nations voted. At last the Jewish people would have its own state! On the fifth day of Iyar, May 14, 1948, Israel declared itself an independent country called **Medinat Yisrael**, the State of Israel.

The very next day, Israel was attacked by five Arab armies. Although Israel had only a small army and a few airplanes, the tiny Jewish state defended itself. The war was won!

For the first time in almost two thousand years, there was a Jewish state where Hebrew was the language spoken by the people. Jews were free to worship and celebrate and to govern themselves.

RETURNING TO ISRAEL

From all over the world, Jews came to Israel. Those who had survived the

Holocaust fled from Europe to begin new lives. Others came from Arab lands, from South America, and from the United States.

Some Jews settled in cities like Tel Aviv, Jerusalem, and Haifa. Some went to live on **kibbutzim**, small communities where people work and live together.

AN ANCIENT LANGUAGE COMES TO LIFE

Teaching Jews from all over the world to speak Hebrew was important. In the early 1900s Eliezer Ben Yehudah modernized Hebrew so that it could become a language to be used in everyday living. Later, a special school called an **ulpan** was created to teach Hebrew to new immigrants.

Today, most of the signs, newspapers, and school books in Israel are printed in Hebrew. On television and in the movies Hebrew is spoken. The Hebrew language lives again in our ancient land.

143

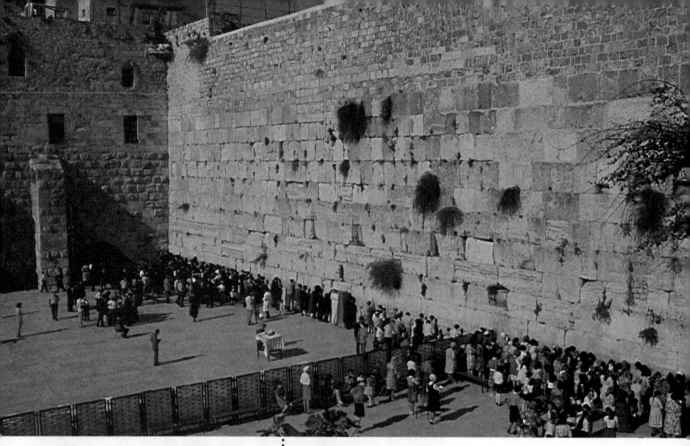

The Temple in Jerusalem was destroyed in the year 70 C.E. But part of the stone wall that surrounded the Temple still stands today. It is called the **Kotel**, or the Western Wall. When you go to Israel, you can pray there with Jews from all over the world.

There is a legend that once, long ago, in the Land of Israel, two brothers had farms right next to one another.

During the harvest one brother thought,
"I will bring extra grain to my brother since he has a family and needs more than I do."

So in the middle of the night he carried a big bag of grain to his brother's field.

That very same night the second brother thought,

"My brother has no family and no one to care for him. I will bring him some of my grain."

And he carried a big bag of grain to his brother's field.

As the two brothers were carrying the bags of grain, they met. They realized that each one was trying to take care of the other. They embraced.

When God saw the love and peace between the two brothers, God decided that the Temple and the city of Jerusalem would be built on this very place. Jerusalem means "City of Peace."

CELEBRATION

Every year we celebrate the courage and bravery of the Jews who struggled to create the State of Israel. Israelis celebrate with parades, flags, and dancing and singing in the streets.

MAKE A MAGEN DAVID

When Israel became a state, a flag was needed. The symbol chosen for the Israeli flag was the Magen David.

The Magen David is a six-pointed star. It appears on Kiddush cups, on jewelry, and on the outside of synagogues.

Connect the dots on the flag to make the Magen David and the stripes. Color them with a blue crayon and you will have made your own Israeli flag.

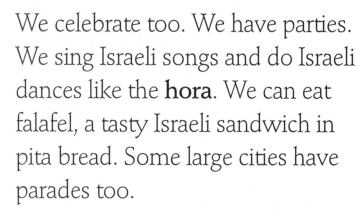

We celebrate too. We have parties. We sing Israeli songs and do Israeli dances like the **hora**. We can eat falafel, a tasty Israeli sandwich in pita bread. Some large cities have parades too.

All celebrations of Yom Ha'atzma'ut include the singing of **Hatikvah**, "The Hope." It is the national anthem of the Jewish State.

HATIKVAH הַתִּקְוָה

As long as within the heart	כָּל עוֹד בַּלֵּבָב פְּנִימָה
a Jewish spirit is still alive	נֶפֶשׁ יְהוּדִי הוֹמִיָּה
and the eyes look eastward toward Zion	וּלְפַאֲתֵי מִזְרָח קָדִימָה עַיִן לְצִיּוֹן צוֹפִיָּה
our hope is not lost	עוֹד לֹא אָבְדָה תִקְוָתֵנוּ
the hope of two thousand years	הַתִּקְוָה שְׁנוֹת אַלְפַּיִם
to be a free nation in our land	לִהְיוֹת עַם חָפְשִׁי בְּאַרְצֵנוּ
in the land of Zion and Jerusalem.	אֶרֶץ צִיּוֹן וִירוּשָׁלָיִם.

MY HOLIDAY DICTIONARY

ALIYAH the act of going to live in Israel—we also use this term when someone is called up to say the Torah blessings—aliyah means "going up"

HATIKVAH Hebrew for "The Hope," the national anthem of Israel

THEODOR HERZL the man who urged Jews around the world to live in Israel

HORA an Israeli folk dance

KIBBUTZIM small communities in Israel where people live and work together

KOTEL the part of the stone wall that surrounded the ancient Temple and still stands in Jerusalem today

MAGEN DAVID a six-pointed star found on the Israeli flag

MEDINAT YISRAEL Hebrew for the "State of Israel"

ULPAN a school which teaches the Hebrew language to immigrants in Israel

ZIONISM the belief that Jews should have their own country

Tishre תִּשְׁרֵי

Ḥeshvan חֶשְׁוָן

Kislev כִּסְלֵו

Tevet טֵבֵת

Shevat שְׁבָט

Adar אֲדָר

Nisan נִיסָן

Iyar אִיָּר

Sivan 6 סִיוָן

Tammuz תַּמּוּז

Av אָב

Elul אֱלוּל

The Torah is a tree of life to those who hold fast, and all who cling to it find happiness.

BOOK OF PROVERBS 3:18

If someone took your bicycle, that person would be told, "It's not right to steal." If someone told your teacher that you caused trouble in the lunch room when you didn't, that person would be told, "It's not right to lie."

שָׁבוּעוֹת

SHAVUOT

Rules like not stealing and not lying come from a set of laws that were given to us by God. They teach us how to lead honest and good lives. Jews have been following God's teachings for three thousand years. These laws are so important that we celebrate the day they were given to us with a holiday called Shavuot.

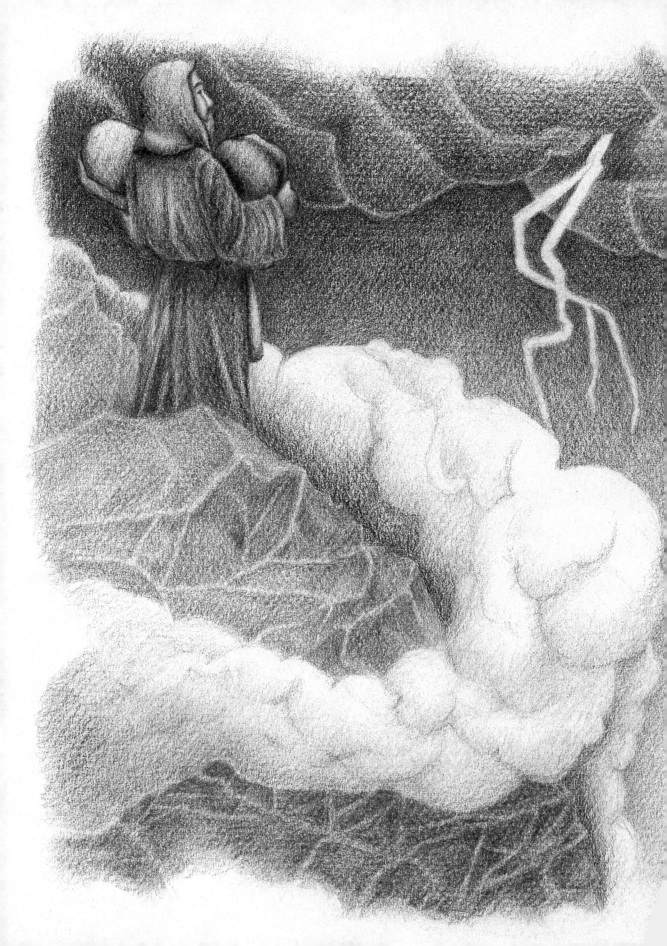

THE GIFT OF TORAH

More than three thousand years ago, God freed us from slavery in Egypt. You have already learned that on Passover we celebrate our freedom from slavery. But people need more than freedom. People need to know how to live as free people.

Seven weeks after we left Egypt, God brought us to a mountain in the Sinai desert. The Torah tells us that the mountain was covered with smoke. Thunder crashed and lightning flashed in the sky. God called Moses to the top of **Mount Sinai.** There Moses stayed for forty days and forty nights. God taught Moses how the Jewish people should live. And God gave the Torah to Moses so that the Jewish people would learn how to live.

Look closely at this cracked mountaintop. Some people believe that this is the very place where Moses received the Ten Commandments.

THE TEN COMMANDMENTS

There is a story that when the Jewish people received the Torah, all the thunder and lightning stopped. There was silence everywhere. Not a bird chirped. Not a lion roared. No person even whispered. Then the **Ten Commandments** were given in a great voice:

1 I am Adonai your God who brought you out of Egypt. You shall have no other gods beside me.

2 You shall not make any idols or worship them.

3 You shall not swear falsely.

4 Remember the Sabbath day and make it holy.

5 Honor your father and your mother.

6 You shall not murder.

7 You shall not commit adultery.

8 You shall not steal.

9 You shall not bear false witness against your neighbor.

10 You shall not be envious of anything that belongs to your neighbor.

There is a legend that when Moses was on Mount Sinai, the Jewish people waited anxiously for his return. When they saw Moses coming down the mountain they could see that he was sad. "What is wrong?" asked the people. Moses said, "God wishes to give us a wonderful gift. It is called the Torah. But God will not give us this gift unless we can show that we will use it wisely."

The people thought long and hard. First they offered jewelry with rubies and emeralds, because they thought that would show God how much they wanted the Torah. But God said that the Torah was more precious than all the jewels in the world.

The people thought again. Finally, a very old and wise man said, "God has offered us the great wisdom of the Torah. What do we do with the wisest things we know?"

Shavuot celebrates two important events: the harvesting of the first fruits, Ḥag Habikkurim, and the giving of the Torah. This happy holiday comes at the end of spring, just before the long hot days of summer. It is a time to be glad for the goodness of life and for God's gifts to us.

"We teach them to our children," replied the people. "Yes," said the old man. "If God will give us the Torah we will promise to teach it faithfully to our children. And our children will teach it to their children."

SHAVUOT SURPRISE

Can you decorate this synagogue with fruit and flowers so that it will be ready for the celebration of Shavuot?

So once again Moses climbed the mountain to speak with God. And when he came down he was carrying the tablets of the Torah.

God gave the Torah to the Jewish people, and to their children, and to their children's children. And the Jewish people have lived by God's teachings ever since.

On Shavuot we read the Ten Commandments from the Torah scroll in the synagogue. The commandments are very important, so we stand while they are read.

In some synagogues people stay up late at night on Shavuot to study the Torah. And in many synagogues teenagers celebrate their progress in religious school with a Confirmation ceremony.

COUNTING THE OMER

Shavuot is important to us not only because we celebrate the giving of the Torah, but for another reason. After our people were freed from slavery, and after they received the commandments at Mount Sinai, the Jews entered the Land of Israel.

Most of our people were farmers in the new land and wheat was a very important crop. Wheat was used for making bread and cereal, just as it is today. Shavuot was a celebration of the

We all look forward to special times. During the week we plan what we will do on the weekend. At the beginning of a meal we wonder what the dessert will be. And at the beginning of Passover, we already begin to look forward to the next holiday, Shavuot.

The word "shavuot" means "weeks," because it comes seven weeks after Passover. We count each day of the seven weeks between Passover and Shavuot. It is as if we were counting the days before we receive a letter from a good friend.

155

OMER COUNTDOWN

For seven weeks after Passover, 49 days, we count the Omer. Shavuot arrives at the end of seven weeks. Figure out how many more days until Shavuot by completing the Omer calendars below.

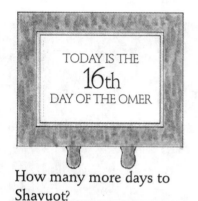

TODAY IS THE
16th
DAY OF THE OMER

How many more days to Shavuot?_____

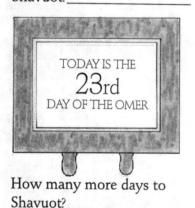

TODAY IS THE
23rd
DAY OF THE OMER

How many more days to Shavuot?_____

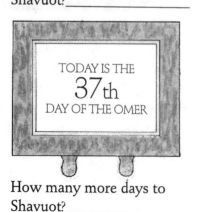

TODAY IS THE
37th
DAY OF THE OMER

How many more days to Shavuot?_____

early summer wheat harvest.

During the seven weeks after Passover, the farmers would carefully tend the plants in the field. They prayed that there would be just the right amount of rain and sunshine so that the harvest would be plentiful.

When the shoots of wheat first appeared, they were short and green. These grew into long thin stalks. The farmers counted the days as the wheat grew. The farmers knew that after forty-nine days, or seven weeks, the wheat would be ready to harvest. Day after day, for seven weeks, they counted. This is called **counting the Omer.**

The gathering of the wheat was so important that the Shavuot celebration was called "the festival of the harvest." At the end of the harvest the farmers brought the first fruits to the Temple in

Jerusalem as an offering to God. So they also called Shavuot, "the festival of the first fruits," Ḥag Habikkurim.

From all over the Land of Israel the Jewish people journeyed to the Temple in Jerusalem. Shavuot is one of the three pilgrimage festivals called *shalosh regalim*.

The farmers traveled on stony, dusty roads. Musicians came along, playing flutes and drums. Bells jingled with silvery sounds.

Each farmer carried a basket filled with the first fruits of the harvest. There were soft ripe figs and sticky-sweet dates. Honey from beehives and ripe grapes from the vine were also brought. There was bread baked with flour made from the new wheat.

When the farmers reached Jerusalem they brought their baskets to the Temple. These first fruits were their gifts to God.

FILL IN THE MISSING WORD

Answer each of the questions below by writing the word in the spaces next to the correct number.

1. A very important crop to the Israelites was

_____.

2. The farmers watched the wheat for _____ weeks.

3. Wheat was used to make loaves of _____.

4. Farmers brought a _____ of fruit to the Temple.

5. The farmers prayed for rain and _____.

1. ☐ __ __ __ __

2. __ ☐ __ __ __

3. __ __ ☐ __ __

4. __ __ __ ☐ __ __

5. ☐ __ __

Use the letters in the boxes above to complete the sentence below.

The Hebrew word Shavuot means

__ __ __ __ __
 1   2   3   4   5

WORD PUZZLE

Circle all the words that are a part of the holiday Shavuot. Below are a list of words to help you.

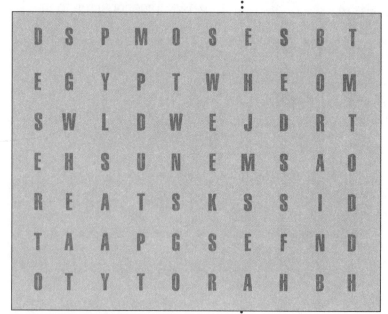

D	S	P	M	O	S	E	S	B	T
E	G	Y	P	T	W	H	E	O	M
S	W	L	D	W	E	J	D	R	T
E	H	S	U	N	E	M	S	A	O
R	E	A	T	S	K	S	S	I	D
T	A	A	P	G	S	E	F	N	D
O	T	Y	T	O	R	A	H	B	H

- WHEAT
- TORAH
- MOSES
- WEEKS
- EGYPT
- DESERT
- RAIN
- SUN

It was their way of thanking God for the food that grew from the earth.

Today in Israel there are often parades on Shavuot. Children carry baskets of fruit to remind us of the time when our ancestors carried the first fruits of summer to the Temple in Jerusalem.

A LAND OF MILK AND HONEY

We remember the harvest of long ago and celebrate the Shavuot holiday by decorating our homes and the synagogue with flowers and plants. It is also customary to eat foods made with milk and cheese, especially blintzes and cheese cake. In the synagogue we read the Book of Ruth and we say prayers of thanks to God for all the good things God has given us.

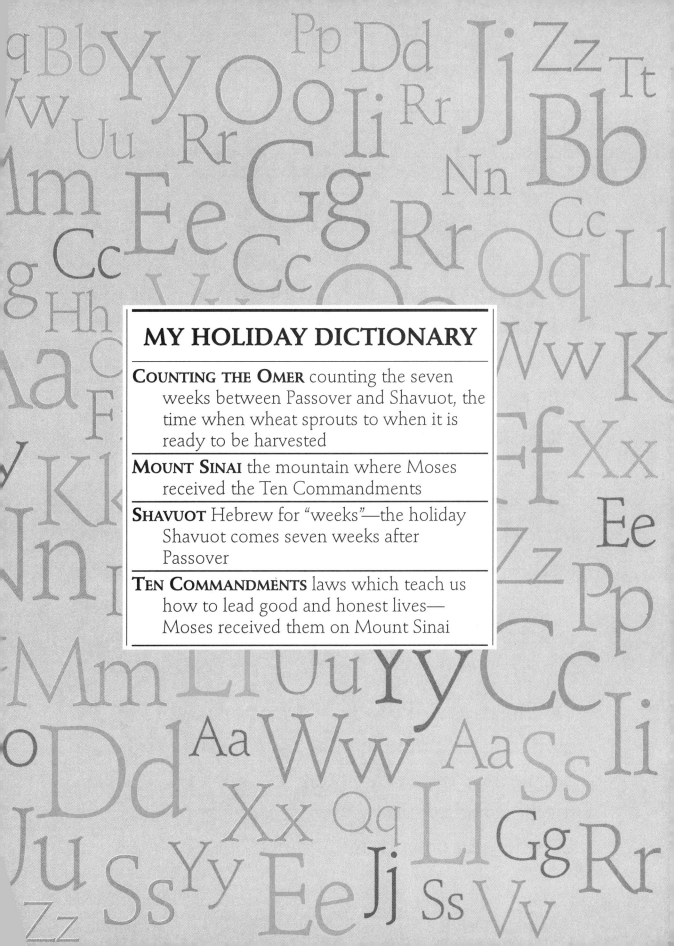

MY HOLIDAY DICTIONARY

COUNTING THE OMER counting the seven weeks between Passover and Shavuot, the time when wheat sprouts to when it is ready to be harvested

MOUNT SINAI the mountain where Moses received the Ten Commandments

SHAVUOT Hebrew for "weeks"—the holiday Shavuot comes seven weeks after Passover

TEN COMMANDMENTS laws which teach us how to lead good and honest lives— Moses received them on Mount Sinai

CELEBRATING TOGETHER

You have learned all about our Jewish holidays. During the year, you have celebrated with your family and friends at home and in the synagogue. Each year you will be able to enjoy these wonderful days again and again, year after year.

When you celebrate, remember that Jews all over the world are also enjoying these same holidays. Think of your grandmother who may live in another state. She lights Ḥanukkah candles just as you do. Your cousin in Israel asks the four questions at the Passover seder just like you. And when you hear the sound of the shofar on Rosh Hashanah, you can be sure that Jews in Russia, France, and Mexico are also welcoming the New Year with sweet honey and crunchy apples.

Our holidays make us feel connected not only to our own families, but to Jews all over the world. Our people have been celebrating some of these holidays for thousands of years. Our holidays bring us closer together, not only to one another, but to God.